D1555263

Intermediate Sanctions
in Overcrowded Times

Advisor in Criminal Justice to Northeastern University Press
GILBERT GEIS

Intermediate Sanctions in Overcrowded Times

Edited by

Michael Tonry

Kate Hamilton

Northeastern University Press   *Boston*

Northeastern University Press

Library of Congress Cataloging-in-Publication Data

Intermediate sanctions in overcrowded times / edited by Michael Tonry,
Kate Hamilton.
p.   cm.
Includes bibliographical references and index.
ISBN 1-55553-221-7 (alk. paper)
1. Alternatives to imprisonment.   2. Prisons—Overcrowding.
3. Jails—Overcrowding.   I. Tonry, Michael H.   II. Hamilton, Kate.
HV9276.5.I574   1995
364.6'8—dc20   94-40529

Designed by David Ford

Composed in Plantin by Coghill Composition Corporation, Richmond,
Virginia. Printed and bound by Edwards Brothers, Inc., Ann Arbor,
Michigan. The paper is Glatfelter Offset, an acid-free stock.

MANUFACTURED IN THE UNITED STATES OF AMERICA
99   98   97   96   95   5   4   3   2   1

Contents

Contents

Contents

Contents

Contributors

Terry L. Baumer is associate professor of public and environmental affairs at Indiana University, Indianapolis.

Michael Brown is assistant professor of criminal justice at Ball State University, Muncie, Indiana.

Paul C. Friday is professor of criminal justice at the University of North Carolina at Charlotte.

Brian Gormally is deputy director of the Northern Ireland Association for the Care and Resettlement of Offenders, Belfast.

Sally T. Hillsman is vice president for research at the National Center for State Courts in Williamsburg, Virginia.

John J. Larivee is executive director of the Crime and Justice Foundation, Boston, Massachusetts.

J. Robert Lilly is professor of sociology at Northern Kentucky University.

Douglas C. McDonald is a sociologist at Abt Associates, Inc., a policy research organization in Cambridge, Massachusetts.

Kieran McEvoy is information officer of the Northern Ireland Association for the Care and Resettlement of Offenders, Belfast.

Gill McIvor is research fellow at the Social Work Research Centre, University of Stirling, Scotland.

Doris Layton MacKenzie is associate professor of criminology at the Institute of Criminal Justice and Criminology, University of Maryland.

George Mair is principal research officer in the Home Office Research and Planning Unit, London.

Marc Mauer is assistant director of The Sentencing Project in Washington, D.C.

Michael G. Maxfield is associate professor of public and environmental affairs at Indiana University, Bloomington.

Contributors

David Moxon is principal research officer in the Home Office Research and Planning Unit in London.

Dale G. Parent is senior analyst at Abt Associates, Inc., a policy research organization in Cambridge, Massachusetts.

Joan Petersilia is professor of criminology at the University of California, Irvine, and former director of the Criminal Justice Program at RAND, Santa Monica, California.

Timothy Roche is a criminal-justice consultant in Alexandria, Virginia.

Dennis S. Schrantz is executive director of the Office of Community Corrections in Lansing, Michigan.

Mary K. Shilton is a criminal-justice consultant in Alexandria, Virginia.

Susan Turner is senior researcher in the Criminal Justice Program at RAND, Santa Monica, California.

Mark S. Umbreit is assistant professor of social work at the University of Minnesota.

Thomas Weigend is professor of law at the University of Cologne, Germany.

Elmar Weitekamp is professor of criminology at the Eberhard-Karls University Institute of Criminology in Tübingen, Germany.

Richard Will is president of Archaeological Research Consultants, Inc., in Ellsworth, Maine.

Matthew Yeager is a consulting criminologist in Ottawa, Canada.

Preface

Intermediate Sanctions in Overcrowded Times is a play on words. With a prison population that has tripled since 1980, upwards of forty state prison systems subject to federal court orders related to crowding, and no end in sight to politicians' calls for still greater use of imprisonment, these are overcrowded times in American prisons and jails, and the crowding and related costs provide the major impetus to development of intermediate sanctions. In addition, all of the articles in this book first appeared in *Overcrowded Times*, a bimonthly journal that specializes in coverage of research and policy developments concerning community-based corrections programs, sentencing reform, and initiatives aimed at reducing America's overreliance on imprisonment as a penal sanction.

From its inception, *Overcrowded Times* has been supported by the Justice Program of the Edna McConnell Clark Foundation, the only major national foundation that has shown continuing interest in criminal justice and corrections policy. The aim is to make reliable, authoritative information on important research and program developments available to policymakers, practitioners, and researchers. Articles on research are written in nontechnical language for a nonspecialist audience, but the writers are generally among the best-informed American and English researchers who specialize in the articles' subjects.

Because crime and punishment present similar challenges in most Western countries, developments in many countries are covered. In the past twenty years, imports and exports of corrections programs have been common. American and English experiments with day fines were efforts to import a sanction in wide and successful use in Germany and Scandinavia. English experiments with electronic monitoring were influenced in part by aggressive American adoption of that spreading technology. American experiments with community service were inspired by extensive English experimentation with community service orders in the early 1970s and their eventual nationwide adoption. Likewise, the first well-known day-reporting center, in Massachusetts, was a deliberate effort to adapt English "day centres" to an American environment.

Much of the information discussed in *Overcrowded Times*, and in this book, is not otherwise generally available in the United States. Many articles report the findings of major evaluations of innovative programs. Much corrections evaluation research is funded by the federal government and carried out by researchers who are dependent on a continuing flow of grant-supported work. Once one project is over and another begun, little time is available to convert final reports into books or articles. Government research agencies publish only a tiny fraction of the final reports they receive. As a result, important work languishes in government file cabinets and is little known except through word-of-mouth by specialists.

Important research findings concerning English developments are little more available, but for a different reason. Much of the most ambitious research is carried out by professional researchers employed by the Home Office. Reports are published by Her Majesty's Stationery Office, but they are expensive and tend to be available in the United States only in major research libraries. To remedy that problem, *Overcrowded Times* regularly commissions senior Home Office researchers to prepare short summaries of their work (for example, on day fines, day-reporting centers, electronic monitoring) for an American audience.

Except for minor stylistic editing, articles are published in this book as they appeared in *Overcrowded Times*. We are grateful to writers for their cooperation and to the Justice Program of the Edna McConnell Clark Foundation and its director, Kenneth Schoen, for their support of *Overcrowded Times*.

So much for our aims, method, and scope. Readers will have to judge for themselves whether the effort to publish short, timely, readable articles on intermediate sanctions in overcrowded times has been worthwhile and successful.

Introduction

There is nothing conceptually or theoretically new about intermediate sanctions. Nor is there anything surprising in the notion that some penal sanctions should be more burdensome and restrictive than probation and less burdensome and restrictive than imprisonment. No schoolchild would be surprised to learn that serious misconduct can result in substantial penalties, that moderately serious misconduct can result in moderately serious penalties, and that trivial misconduct generally results in little or no penalty.

Only in recent decades have the ideas become widespread that no sanction less burdensome than imprisonment counts, and that the sentencing judge's choice is between doing nothing, imposing "mere probation," or sending a miscreant to prison. In the mid-nineteenth century, when John Augustus, anticipating probation, began his volunteer supervision of young offenders released to his custody, it seemed obvious that the nature of the supervision and the offender's obligations would vary from case to case. In the 1950s and 1960s, the framers of the American Law Institute's *Model Penal Code* (1962)—the basis for revised criminal codes in more than half the states—drafted the code's sentencing and corrections provisions. It seemed obvious then that prison sentences would be reserved for the most serious crimes and criminals and that for the others the conditions of community-based sentences would vary with offenders' needs for assistance, supervision, and control.

Two major changes with roots in the 1960s and 1970s have led to the view that only prison counts and to the need, if that view is to be overcome, to promote sanctions intermediate between prison and probation. First, beginning with Barry Goldwater's use of "law and order" as an issue in the 1964 presidential election, conservative politicians have consistently disparaged their opponents as "soft on crime" and have suggested that punitive policies featuring vastly greater use of imprisonment will make a safer society. The push in 1994 for "three strikes and you're out" laws that require life sentences for people convicted of a second or third felony is merely the latest example.

More than twenty-five years of such policies have not demonstrably made the United States a safer place. Between 1980 and 1993, for example, the number of people confined in American prisons and jails tripled (Bureau of Justice Statistics 1994); between 1979 and 1991, violent crime rates increased by 38 percent and property crimes by 2 percent (Maguire, Pastore, and Flanagan 1993). In England, Canada, and the United States, time and again, often under conservative governments, distinguished advisory committees have questioned the effectiveness of harsh crime control policies. The Committee on Justice and the Solicitor General of the Canadian House of Commons, headed by a member of conservative prime minister Brian Mulroney's party, observed in a 1993 report that "the United States affords a glaring example of the limited impact that criminal justice responses may have on crime. . . . If locking up those who violate the law contributed to safer societies, then the United States should be the safest country in the world." Likewise, the National Academy of Sciences Panel on the Understanding and Control of Violent Behavior (Reiss and Roth 1993), funded by the Department of Justice during the Reagan and Bush administrations, noted that the average lengths of prison sentences for violent crimes tripled between 1975 and 1989. The panel posed this question in its 1993 report: "What effect has increasing the prison population had on levels of violent crime?" Its answer: "Apparently, very little." An English government white paper, *Crime, Justice, and Protecting the Public*, issued by Margaret Thatcher's Home Office in 1990, reached a similar conclusion.

Although there is thus little basis for believing that harsh punishment policies make a safer world, appeals to voters' fears and frustrations demonstrably do win elections. This is exemplified by George Bush's use of Willie Horton in the 1988 presidential election to suggest that Michael Dukakis was "soft on crime." It is easy to seize the low ground in political debates about crime control. This is why candidates often compete to establish who is tougher, and seldom argue— except by epithet and declamation—about the comparative effectiveness of alternative policy choices. It is why President Clinton in 1993 and 1994 was often applauded by pundits for "taking the crime issue away from the Republicans" by his support for tougher penalties, more capital crimes, and increased federal funds for police and prisons.

The second development that has prompted interest in intermediate sanctions is the displacement of rehabilitative rationales for punishment by retributive "desert" rationales. The sentencing reform movement of the last twenty-five years had diverse origins—research casting doubt on the effectiveness of treatment programs (Sechrest, White, and Brown 1979); liberals' concern to reduce unwarranted sentencing disparities and reduce scope for racial and class bias (American Friends Service Committee 1971); proceduralists' hope to enhance judicial accountability by establishing standards for sentencing (Frankel 1972; Morris 1974); and conservatives' aspiration to make sentences tougher by making it harder for judges to impose "lenient" sentences (van den Haag 1975; Wilson 1975).

The policy agendas of the different reform proponents converged on proposals that standards be set for sentences and that judges be accountable for adhering to them. Almost inevitably, given the loss of credibility of rehabilitative justifications for sentences, new sentencing standards were based largely on the severity of the defendants' crimes and sometimes their records of past criminality. Desert theorists like Andrew von Hirsch (1976) argued that a just sentencing system must satisfy principles of proportionality in which the defendant's punishment is closely scaled to the seriousness of his crime. Even atheoretical sentencing systems that explicitly rejected the need for philosophical premises, like the U.S. Sentencing Commission's guidelines, closely proportioned sentencing standards to commonsense notions of offense severity. The federal guidelines, for example, establish forty-three different levels of offense severity (U.S. Sentencing Commission 1994).

Together, the political pressures for toughness and the logic of proportionality have created the need for intermediate sanctions. Just as in the 1970s liberal and conservative points of view combined to support creation of systems of structured sentencing discretion, so in the 1990s they converge to support creation of continuums of sanctions scaled to the severity of offenses and to the public safety risks individual offenders pose. Many liberals promote intermediate sanctions as a means to divert people from prison or secure their earlier release, often because of beliefs that modern use of imprisonment is excessive, cruel, ineffective, and too costly. For intermediate sanctions to be seen as credible in a punitive political environment they must be seen as burdensome and restrictive; to be seen as just, they must be scaled to offense severity (Morris and Tonry 1990).

Many conservatives, by contrast, argue that we need more, not less, imprisonment; but in the face of rapidly increasing corrections budgets and taxpayer resistance to spending on more prisons, they often see intermediate sanctions as a device for imposing burdens and controls on people for whom prisons lack space (Thornburgh 1991).

Since the early 1980s, pressures from the left and the right—from concern to reduce prison use and to augment it, from concern to save offenders unnecessary suffering and to save taxpayers money—have combined into broad-based support for intermediate sanctions. As a result, they have proliferated.

Beginning with much-publicized programs in the early

1980s in Georgia, where judges ostensibly sentenced prison-bound offenders to intensive probation supervision rather than imprisonment (Erwin 1987), and in New Jersey, where judges released low-risk prisoners early into intensive parole supervision (Pearson 1988), intensive supervision programs, commonly known as ISP programs, soon spread to every state and most counties. Beginning with much-publicized programs in the mid-1980s in Florida, where judges ostensibly sentenced prison-bound offenders to house arrest (Baird and Wagner 1990), and in Oklahoma, where corrections officials released inmates early into house arrest (Meachum 1986), house arrest soon spread to every state and most counties.

And so it was with every other recently invented or reinvented intermediate sanction. Electronic monitoring of probationers and parolees began in the mid-1980s with small pilot programs in Florida, Kentucky, Oregon, and California, generally involving fewer than fifty offenders (Morris and Tonry 1990); by the mid-1990s tens of thousands were estimated to be subject to electronic monitoring. A pilot project in the use of day fines—monetary penalties scaled both to the seriousness of the offense and to the offender's means—began in Staten Island, New York, in the late 1980s (Hillsman 1990). By the mid-1990s day-fine projects had spread to at least another half-dozen jurisdictions. Boot camps—short-term prisons featuring strict discipline and hard physical labor, ostensibly to be used in lieu of longer sentences to conventional prisons—began in a few southern states in the mid-1980s and by the mid-1990s had spread to nearly thirty states (MacKenzie 1993). Day-reporting centers, based on English experience with "day centres" to which offenders were sentenced during working hours, began in Massachusetts and Minnesota in the mid-1980s; these had spread to all regions of the country by the mid-1990s (Parent 1991). Organized community service programs began a bit earlier, in California in the 1960s (Morris and Tonry 1990), and were moved forward by a celebrated pilot project conducted by the Vera Institute of Justice in New

York City (McDonald 1986). They have since been adopted in every state. A similar story could be told of the dispersion of victim-offender mediation programs (Umbreit and Coates 1993).

It is important to reiterate that little of this is new. English judges were diverting offenders from the gallows to intermediate sanctions of transportation to Georgia three hundred years ago and to Australia somewhat later. Experimentation with intensive probation was widespread in the 1950s and 1960s (although on the different rationale that smaller caseloads would permit officers to provide more extensive and effective rehabilitative assistance). Day reporting is more systematic but little different in principle from halfway houses and intermittent day- or nighttime confinement, both of which have been widely used for at least forty years. Community service has been in widespread use in England since the early 1970s; day fines have been imposed in Scandinavia since the 1920s and in Germany since the early 1970s. House arrest is more widespread but no different from the not uncommon probation conditions in earlier times stipulating that probationers be in their homes when not at work or in transit to and from work. Electronic monitoring is new but is only a technology used to buttress supervision.

New or not, intermediate sanctions have proliferated and been the subject of considerable numbers of evaluations. There have never been enough evaluations and they are seldom adequately funded, but we have learned a fair amount from them. First, the principal reason new programs fail is that they are poorly implemented, with insufficient planning, money, or support. "Implementation failure" is probably the single most common finding of evaluations of intermediate sanctions.

Second, although many new programs are promoted on claims that they will divert offenders from prison, reduce recidivism rates, and save taxpayers money, many fail to achieve any of these claims. One serious problem, and the reason preceding paragraphs often refer to programs that "ostensibly" serve prison-bound offenders, is that judges often sentence to these programs offenders who would otherwise have received a less restrictive community sentence. By contrast, RAND Corporation evaluation research on ISP programs purportedly randomly assigning prison-bound offenders to prison or ISP found that judges so often refused to follow the random assignments that the experimental evaluations could not be carried out (Petersilia and Turner 1993). Offenders in the much-ballyhooed Georgia ISP program, for a converse example, had remarkably low rearrest and reconviction rates; eventually it became clear that judges were principally sentencing exceedingly low-risk offenders to the program rather than higher-risk, prison-bound offenders (Morris and Tonry 1990). Reasonable people differ in their views of the appropriateness of that practice. Critics disparage it as "net-widening" that further diminishes more offenders' liberty. Others see the practice as an understandable reaction by judges who thought prison too severe for some offenders and therefore reluctantly sentenced them to ordinary probation, which they considered too mild a penalty; for such offenders the new program may look like an appropriate midlevel sanction. However the practice is assessed, the effect is that many offenders sentenced to new "diversion" programs cost the jurisdiction more than if an ordinary sentence had been imposed.

Net-widening is aggravated by another characteristic of many intermediate sanctions. Because new programs must be tough to be credible, they often enforce conditions vigorously; in many programs, 40 to 50 percent of offenders fail to comply with conditions, have their participation revoked, and are ejected, usually into a jail or prison term. Of course, it costs money to operate the new programs, to process the revocations, and to hold those ejected in jails and prisons. When many of those sentenced to jail for breach of conditions turn out to have been diverted from nonintensive ordinary

Introduction

probation into the intermediate sanction and then ejected into jail, the per-capita cost of handling them increases greatly. Dale Parent's article (1993) on the effectiveness of boot camps demonstrates that such camps are likely to save money only if they have very low net-widening rates and low-to-moderate failure rates, conditions that few boot camps meet. Similar analyses have been done for other intermediate sanctions (Morris and Tonry 1990). Good intermediate sanctions programs are expensive to operate. For example, if a jurisdiction's per-capita annual costs for prison, ISP, and ordinary probation are $25,000, $12,000, and $1,500, respectively, it does not take much net-widening or terribly high failure rates for the intermediate sanction to lose its cost advantages.

Third, a consistent finding from evaluations of intermediate sanctions is that offenders sentenced to them tend to have no lower (but also no higher) recidivism rates for new crimes than do apparently comparable offenders sentenced to harsher penalties. Typically, however, failure rates are higher for breaches of conditions not involving new crimes. This is the consequence of the intensiveness of supervision in intermediate sanctions and operators' enthusiasm for strict enforcement. Offenders sentenced to intermediate sanctions probably do not commit more technical violations of conditions than do other offenders; they are simply more likely to be caught.

Do these findings mean that intermediate sanctions are a failed innovation? Apparently yes, but actually no. The argument for failure is based on the inability of many programs to achieve their proponents' goals of diversion of offenders from prison, reduced recidivism rates, and net cost savings. Most proponents of such programs, I believe, offered their predictions of success in good faith. In retrospect, the folk wisdom that "most offers that appear too good to be true probably aren't" should have been applied to many intermediate sanctions. The problem of extensive net-widening should have been foreseen, and in many quarters was. The problem of high failure rates should have been foreseen, and occasionally

8

was. The high costs of processing condition violators and reincarcerating them should have been foreseen, but seldom were.

A decade ago program proponents often predicted major cost savings by comparing the per-capita annual direct operating costs of a new program with the per-capita annual cost of a prison bed. This was an inadequate comparison for a number of reasons. It failed to adjust for different average times in prison and in the new program. Diverting a prisoner from a three-month jail term in a $20,000-per-year bed (cost: $5,000) to a twelve-month ISP program at $6,000 per year represents no savings. In addition, the comparison of per-capita prison or jail costs with per-capita costs of new programs was often misleading. The marginal per-capita costs of squeezing two or ten more offenders into a prison is quite low and considerably less than the average per-capita costs of new programs. Only if an entire prison or prison wing were closed or not built because of intermediate sanctions would the per-capita comparison of average annual costs be appropriate. The most fundamental oversight, however, was neglect of the costs of police, court, prosecutorial, jail, and prison operations required to process recidivists and condition violators.

We now understand these problems and are considerably more sophisticated in thinking about new sanctions programs and in evaluating them. Many of the newly faddish sanctions have followed a similar cycle. It begins with reformers and bureaucratic entrepreneurs who propose a new program and believe in its likely success. Reservations offered by others are cast aside as unduly pessimistic, and possible problems are overlooked or downplayed. From the perspective of a local probation manager, for example, the prosecutorial, judicial, and jail costs of processing violators come out of other agencies' budgets, are not the concern of the probation office, and are therefore easy to overlook. Often, early pilot projects, seldom carefully evaluated, appear to their operators to be a success. The Georgia ISP program mentioned earlier is an example. Replications follow, as eventually do more rigorous evaluations. The evaluations generally conclude that recidivism is not perceptibly improved or worsened (except for technical violations), that half or more of the participating offenders were not really prison-bound, and that cost savings are nonexistent or have been exaggerated.

Neither this pattern of program development nor the patterns of findings on net-widening, recidivism, and costs need be as disheartening as they may appear, for they offer three guides toward increased, cost-effective use of intermediate sanctions. First, the situational and psychological pressures on judges to sentence probation-bound offenders to programs designed for prison-bound offenders are powerful and are likely to be overcome only by counterpressure. Fifteen years' experience with sentencing guidelines (often somewhat clumsily referred to as "structured sentencing") instructs that judges' sentencing discretion can be channeled by guidelines into patterns that policymakers set (Tonry 1993). Thus, if judicial inclinations to use intermediate sanctions for people other than those for whom they were intended are to be overcome, sentencing guidelines systems are going to have to be expanded to set standards for intermediate sanctions and to specify which of them are principally intended to be used in lieu of incarceration. A few sentencing commissions have begun nibbling at these issues, but no ambitious schemes have as yet been implemented.

Second, the "no effect on recidivism" finding needs to be seen as at least partly positive. The relevance of rearrest or reconviction rates no better and no worse than those of comparable offenders sent to jail or prison varies with the nature of the offender's crimes and the public safety risks they pose. When the behavior in issue is rape or robbery or homicide, little good can be said about a prison-diversion program that produces no better and and no worse recidivism rates. These are frightening and damaging crimes, and the higher costs of prison are justifiable if a new intermediate sanction cannot offer heightened public safety. So long as offenders who present unacceptable risks of violence are in prison, they are incapacitated from committing new offenses in the community and it is hard to see any gain from releasing them early. Those who will reoffend will do so that much earlier, and it is hard to see why that is a public benefit.

However, when the behavior at issue is property crimes or situational assaults or minor drug trafficking, the calculus may change. No better and no worse recidivism by such offenders offers a much more attractive inducement to reduce the costs to taxpayers and the cruelty to offenders of keeping them in prison. Some will not recidivate at all, and their release to an intermediate sanctions program represents a clear gain in the saving of public resources otherwise expended on their imprisonment. Some will recidivate, but so long as they do not present high risks for violent criminality, the social costs will not be great and the trade-off between economic and humanitarian savings from reduced incarceration often will outweigh the social costs of the new crimes that would not have been committed had the offender been in prison. This involves acceptance of the occurrence of minor crimes that would not otherwise have happened. Most Western countries as a matter of national policy discourage use of prison sentences for punishment of property offenders, in effect deciding that the social gains from reduced incarceration outweigh the social costs of the resulting crimes.

Despite the public mythology to the contrary, encouraged by disingenuous claims of conservative politicians, American prisons contain many nonviolent offenders who could safely be handled in community-based intermediate sanctions. Former attorney general William Barr, for example, often claims that 95 percent of prisoners are violent or otherwise dangerous offenders (Barr 1992). According to data released by the Department of Justice's Bureau of Justice Statistics for 1991, a year when Barr was attorney general, only 27 percent of persons admitted to state prisons had been convicted of violent crimes (the federal percentage is even smaller) and a third each had been convicted of property and drug offenses. Although some of the remaining 73 percent may have had long criminal records or histories of violence, many could safely be sentenced to intermediate sanctions. Eighteen percent had never before been convicted of a crime and another 18 percent had never been in a prison or jail before (Beck et al. 1993).

Third, we can improve intermediate sanctions' cost-effectiveness by greatly reducing the number and intrusiveness of conditions to which participants are subject and establishing modest but graduated responses to deal with those that are violated. Offenders should of course be forbidden to commit new crimes and should be subject to conditions that are meaningfully related to their crimes. An assaulter who is violent only when he drinks should be forbidden to drink in public and required to participate in alcohol treatment programs with consequences attaching when either condition is violated. A spouse assaulter whose victim remains fearful and who wishes not to see him should be forbidden to contact the victim. By contrast, it makes little sense routinely to impose curfews on all participants and to forbid all participants to consume alcohol or other drugs if those conditions are not importantly related to offenders' past crimes. Many offenders will violate them and the program will be forced to ignore the violations, thereby undermining its own integrity and credibility; or it will respond to them, incurring processing costs and possible jail or prison costs that are unrelated to the program's fundamental mission of reducing or preventing crime.

When violations do occur, responses should be graduated. An arrest for a violent crime or some other serious crime should result in formal prosecution. An arrest for a minor property crime or a drug crime might, the prosecutor willing, result only in a violation hearing and a denial of privileges: for example, a special curfew for a month, a fixed number of hours of community service. A first violation of an appropriate condition might warrant a similar response, with each subsequent violation receiving a sterner reaction, culminating in formal revocation proceedings leading to incarceration.

The principal argument for intermediate sanctions is that they offer a way to development of a continuum of graduated sanctions, most of which fall between prison and probation, which will allow judges to scale the sanctions offenders receive to the seriousness of their crimes and to levels of supervision and control fitted to the offender's risks and needs.

This volume offers an up-to-date and comprehensive survey of recent research and policy developments concerning the most widely used intermediate sanctions, in this country and elsewhere. Many of the writers are the country's leading evaluation researchers on their subjects: Joan Petersilia and Susan Turner on ISP, Sally Hillsman and Susan Turner on day fines, Doris MacKenzie and Dale Parent on boot camps, Mark Umbreit on victim-offender mediation, Michael Maxfield, Terry Baumer, and Robert Lilly on electronic monitoring, Dale Parent and John Larivee on day-reporting centers, Douglas McDonald on community service. Articles on parallel or prior developments in England are written by that country's leading evaluation researchers, including George Mair on day-reporting centers and electronic monitoring, David Moxon on day fines, and Gill McIvor on community service.

Together these articles show both the promise and the challenges of intermediate sanctions. From experience and research, we know how to design, implement, and evaluate intermediate sanctions to avoid past pitfalls and how to structure their use and link their conditions to behavior. If we have the political will, we can operate intermediate sanctions that save money, reduce prison populations, and avoid unnecessary disruption to the lives of offenders and their families, and all without sacrificing important public interests in public safety. The only question is whether we will soon have the political will.

1

MONETARY PENALTIES

Introduction

It seems odd, in a country where economic incentives and rational calculation are so widely celebrated, that monetary penalties play so small a part in punishment of offenders. Although in practice fines are generally set in amounts too small to be commensurate to the seriousness of nontrivial crimes, in principle they can vary from small change to economic capital punishment. Although in practice fines are often collected haphazardly or not at all, in principle they can be collected with the same vigor and solicitude that characterize our friendly neighborhood finance companies. Although in practice increased use of fines seems likely to be unfair to the poor and unduly lenient to the rich, in principle amounts can be tailored to individuals' assets and incomes so as to constitute roughly comparable financial burdens.

In many Western countries, including England, Germany, and Sweden, the fine is the most commonly ordered sanction and is employed for serious property crimes and many violent crimes. Partly this greater use of fines derives from recognition that a fine can serve both deterrent and retributive ends. Partly it derives from less punitive policy climates in those countries and objections to the unnecessary use of incarceration. The Swedish government's Council for Crime Prevention recently observed, for example, "In Sweden short-term imprisonment is nowadays generally considered to be an inappropriate sanction from the social, ethical, and economic points of view" (National Swedish Council for Crime Prevention 1986).

Experience in European countries has shown both that fines can be credible midlevel punishments for use in lieu of incarceration and that they can be implemented in ways that assure both that they are collected and that they are fairly adjusted to offenders' means. Recent German experience demonstrates both propositions. In 1970, on the basis of the "idea that short-term imprisonment does more harm than good" (Weigend 1992, 1993), a penal code amendment was adopted that established a strong statutory presumption against imposition of prison sentences under six months. As a result, though 168,000 such sentences were ordered in 1968, the number fell to 56,000 in 1970 and has continued gradually downward to 48,000 in 1989 (many of which were suspended). In 1975, in order to make use of fines more fair, Germany adopted a system of day fines, patterned on Swedish practice. (The articles by Thomas Weigend tell that story.)

Day fines were introduced in Finland in 1921, in Sweden in 1931, and in Denmark in 1939. They represent an effort simultaneously to adjust fines to the severity of the offender's crime and to his assets and income. Although details vary, most day-fine systems treat one day's disposable income as one day-fine unit. Thus, for a laborer, one day's after-tax-and-social-security income might be $30; for a schoolteacher, it might be $100; for a lawyer, $450. Day-fine units can be scaled to the severity of crimes. A minor theft might be a 3-unit offense, shoplifting 10 units, retail sale of marijuana 20 units, a situational assault 30 units. Thus for the same sale of marijuana, the laborer might be fined $600, the teacher $2,000, and the lawyer $9,000. We have left out lots of details. Most day-fine systems, for example, take account of fixed obligations and basic living expenses, and refinements must make sure that the system does not result in inordinately high fines for trivial crimes (say, $1,500 for littering) or fines that appear economically perverse (say, a $150 fine for $1,000 taken from a merchant's till). Those, however, are soluble details.

America's experience with fines has been much less successful. As a series of surveys in the 1980s by the Vera Institute of Justice demonstrated, fines are imposed much more often than is generally recognized, but almost always for traffic and other minor offenses, and seldom for serious offenses. Many jurisdictions are remarkably inefficient at collecting fines. Sometimes this is because no specialized office exists to collect fines and collection is an unglamorous activity to which officials such as prosecutors, judges, and probation officers assign low priority. Sometimes there is no bureaucratic incentive to invest resources in collection; amounts received are not retained by the courts but are treated as miscellaneous general government revenue. Finally, the entire system for cash payments by offenders is sometimes so convoluted and unrealistic that few take it seriously. Many jurisdictions in recent years have imposed user fees on offenders (for probation supervision, drug tests, electronic monitoring) and have ordered often indigent offenders in addition to pay court costs, restitution, and fines. The aggregate amounts are often so large and payment so improbable that everyone realizes the offender cannot meet his obligations; little or nothing gets paid.

Nonetheless, recent experiments with financial penalties suggest that these penalties can play a larger role in American criminal courts, as the articles in this section by Sally Hillsman and Susan Turner demonstrate. A pilot day-fines project in New York City showed that fines can be collected efficiently, that judges can be persuaded to impose financial penalties on people convicted of serious crimes, and that a system of means-based financial penalties is feasible. The New York example inspired other jurisdictions to experiment with day fines, which in turn led to a series of federally funded demonstration projects and a federally funded evaluation.

In a parallel track, recent experience with day fines in

England and Wales shows both the feasibility and the difficulty of establishing day-fine systems. Although fines are more commonly ordered for nontrivial crimes in England and Wales than in the United States, they are typically imposed in fixed "tariff" amounts and are often criticized for being unduly harsh on impecunious offenders and unduly gentle on the privileged. After a successful and carefully documented pilot project, the Criminal Justice Act 1991 established a national system of "unit fines." As one of the articles by David Moxon demonstrates, the unit-fine system ran into both judicial recalcitrance and implementation problems that led quickly to statutory changes and abandonment of the scheme. There are, however, lessons to be learned. With the luxury of hindsight, the implementation problems could have been foreseen; developers of future such systems should be able to avoid them.

Finally, in many countries, there has been since the 1970s extensive development of victim-offender mediation programs that often result in negotiated restitution orders by which the offender agrees to make regular payments to the victim. These programs are often premised on notions of reparative justice, and reconciliation between offender and victim is often viewed as equally important as the restitution order. The articles by Mark Umbreit chronicle the spread of victim-offender mediation and summarize the findings of the largest evaluation yet undertaken on the effects of such programs on both offenders and victims.

Fines

Day Fines

Sally T. Hillsman

Day fines—fine sentences in which the amount is set in proportion to both the seriousness of the offense and the financial resources of the offender—have long been the sentence of choice in northern Europe for most offenses. The name derives from the practice of using the offender's daily income as the base for setting the fine amount.

Systematic day-fine systems typically rely upon flexible, written guidelines. They are increasingly attractive to American judges, prosecutors, and other criminal justice policymakers who look for a wider range of intermediate penalties that can be scaled to provide appropriate punishment for offenses of varying gravity, while reserving imprisonment for violent and predatory offenses.

The fine has always been an attractive sentence in American courts, and it is used more widely than is generally recognized. The fine's advantages are well known. Fines are unmistakably punitive; they deprive offenders of ill-gotten gain; they are inexpensive to administer; and they provide revenue to cover such things as the cost of collection or compensation to victims. Recent research has supported their deterrent impact: fines are associated with lower rates of recidivism than probation or jail for offenders with equivalent criminal records and current offenses.

Fines have not been used in the United States, particularly as a sole penalty, as frequently or for as wide a range of offenses as in European countries, which share many of our sentencing principles. In Germany, for example, 81 percent of adult offenses and 73 percent of crimes of violence are punished solely by fines. In England, 38 percent of offenses equivalent to our felonies and 39 percent of violent offenses result in fines.

A major impediment in American courts has been the widespread view that poor offenders cannot pay fines and that affluent offenders who do so are buying their way out of more punitive sanctions. Whatever truth there is in this view, however, stems largely from American use of "tariff" systems to set fine amounts. Tariff systems use informal "going rates" to guide judges in setting amounts. Because tariff systems tend to equate equity with consistency, they generally result in fines keyed to the lowest common economic denominator. This tends to limit judges' ability to adjust fines to an individual offender's financial means and to restrict their use of fines to less serious crimes or first offenders.

In contrast, day fines provide courts with greater capacity to vary fine amounts in a systematic and principled way. Day-fine systems accomplish this by a two-step process. First, the judge sentences an offender to a given number of fine units (e.g., 10, 15, or 90), which reflects the appropriate degree of punishment. Courts that rely on day fines have developed informal guidelines or benchmarks that suggest what number (or range) of units is appropriate for crimes of differing gravity.

The second step is to determine the monetary value of these units. Courts typically develop a rough but standardized method for calculating the proportion of a defendant's daily income that they view to be a "fair share" for the purposes of fining.

Using information routinely available from the police, a pretrial agency, probation, or (most often) the defendant, the judge will estimate the defendant's daily income and calculate the day-fine unit value. Multiplication of the number of units by this unit value produces the fine amount.

Since 1988, a day-fine system has been operating successfully in the Criminal Court of Richmond County, Staten

Island, New York. A day-fine program has also been running successfully for over a year in the Maricopa Superior Court in Phoenix, Arizona. In Milwaukee, the day fine was introduced with considerable success as a strategy to reduce high levels of default among low-income offenders. Day-fine projects are under way in Oregon, Iowa, and Connecticut as part of a national demonstration project on "structured fines" sponsored by the Bureau of Justice Assistance. Numerous other jurisdictions are beginning to experiment with the concept, sometimes with encouragement from their state legislatures. In California, for example, legislation authorizes implementation of day-fine pilots.

For more information on day fines, see David Moxon, Mike Sutton, and Carol Hedderman, *Unit Fines: Experiments in Four Courts*; and Laura A. Winterfield and Sally T. Hillsman, *The Effects of Instituting Means-Based Fines in a Criminal Court: The Staten Island Day-Fine Experiment.*

Day Fines in New York
Sally T. Hillsman

The first day fine in the United States was imposed by a judge of the Richmond County Criminal Court in Staten Island, New York, on August 12, 1988. That event was the culmination of an eighteen-month planning process involving the Staten Island bench, prosecutors, public and private defense attorneys, court administrators, and planners and researchers from the Vera Institute of Justice in New York City.

Nearly ten years earlier, Vera researchers and colleagues from the Institute for Court Management had begun studying American and European courts' use and administration of fines. From that process emerged the belief that the European day-fine technique could provide a flexible tool for broader use of the fine as a criminal penalty in American courts. The Staten Island pilot project was designed to test whether the day-fine concept could be adapted to an American context and successfully implemented in a fairly typical American court.

The Staten Island project has demonstrated that the day fine is an attractive, workable sentencing option and has some advantages over the fixed fines traditionally imposed by American courts. In addition, the day fine is attracting increasing attention from practitioners and policymakers around the United States.

PLANNING THE STATEN ISLAND EXPERIMENT

Throughout the United States, lower courts have long been the primary users of fine sentences. The criminal court in Staten Island is no exception; in addition, like many other American lower courts, it sentences a broad range of offenses, both misdemeanors and felonies disposed as misdemeanors. Despite being part of the City of New York, Staten Island typifies many middle-sized, suburban communities characterized by not insubstantial crime problems and significant poverty and unemployment.

The planning group's major task was to develop the two essential components of the day fine. First, the group had to establish a set of sentencing benchmarks to guide judges in selecting appropriate numbers of fine units for offenses of varying severity. They did this by classifying the common offenses for which sentences are imposed in Staten Island according to the degree of seriousness of the specific criminal behaviors typically involved, and then distributing a range of fine units across these offenses.

Second, the planning group crafted a method for giving a monetary value to the fine units on the basis of offenders' daily income net of taxes. To establish the "fair share" of this amount to be available for fining, net daily income is discounted according to the number of dependents an offender has, and then discounted again by one-third (or one-half for those below the poverty line) to bring the finable share to a level the group considered both appropriate and equitable.

Using this method, the day-fine amounts in the Staten Island court could range from a low of $25 for a welfare recipient with three children who was convicted of the least serious offense in the court's jurisdiction, to $4,000 for a single offender with no dependents and a gross annual income of $35,000 who was sentenced for the most serious crime.

Simple, standardized forms aid the Staten Island judges in making the necessary day-fine calculations quickly at the bench, using only a few pieces of information on income and personal characteristics that are readily available from the court's pretrial services agency and from defendants or their counsel. Random verification confirmed that, for the most part, the self-reported information was sufficiently accurate for these sentencing purposes.

IMPLEMENTING THE DAY-FINE EXPERIMENT

Judges in the Staten Island court began using day fines in August 1988; although they had the option of continuing to use traditional fixed fines, day fines were used in 70 percent of the cases fined. The remaining cases were those levied by temporary judges sitting in the court who were unfamiliar with the new system, a few unusual offenses for which the judges had not yet set benchmarks, and several plea bargains in which a prosecutor had negotiated a fixed fine amount.

Overall there was full acceptance of the day-fine system by the bench and the public and private bar. No conflicts arose beyond the usual plea negotiations, and evidence from court records indicates that judges generally set the day fines in accordance with the procedures they had created as part of the planning group. There was no indication that judges were merely reproducing the traditional tariff system by starting with a fixed fine amount and then "backing into" the day-fine units.

The Staten Island project also included an experimental fine collection system for the court. This tested the effects of using a more individualized collection system (personalized payment schedules, notifications, and warnings), and was compared with the court's more traditional system of calendaring cases each time a payment was due and routinely issuing (unserved) warrants when the offender failed to appear in court.

An experimental "fine office" was established, staffed by a Vera Institute fines officer and an administrative assistant who maintained a PC-based tracking system developed by the planners. For the experimental period, this system operated parallel to the court's traditional system and handled a portion of the day-fine cases.

Again, implementation was smooth. Court administrators were extremely helpful in establishing the new office. In addition to setting fine payment schedules, tracking payments, and notifying and warning fined offenders, the fines officer also returned fined cases to court for judicial decisions about reducing fine amounts or resentencing. The fines officer provided documentation on the person's payment record and current circumstances.

EVALUATING THE DAY-FINE EXPERIMENT

The Vera Institute research department is conducting a full-scale evaluation of the Staten Island experiment; the findings are not yet in. Vera planners and the court have been collecting program data that provide preliminary evidence for assessing the experiment.

Despite the initial complexities of implementing a new fining system, fine use appears stable in the Staten Island court. Day fines, therefore, have not been a disincentive to the use of fine sentences, but they also do not appear to have encouraged greater fine use in this court, at least not during the transitional period.

The impact of introducing the day-fine method can be seen most clearly in the increased variability of fine amounts and in their overall size. Under the court's traditional tariff system, fine amounts clustered at a limited number of specific dollar amounts; under the day-fine system, the amounts vary widely.

Furthermore, total fine amounts levied by the court rose, and would have risen higher had not the larger day fines set by the court been "capped" by the state's low statutory fine ceilings. (Although the day-fine system devised by the Staten Island court permitted a maximum fine of $4,000, the maximum statutory fine in New York State's lower courts is $1,000.) Under the court's day-fine system, the uncapped fine amounts set by the judges rose approximately 18 percent over previous tariff amounts. However, after the judges capped all day-fine amounts that rose above the statutory maximum at the permissible limit, fine amounts rose about 8 percent. The New York State legislature will soon consider a bill to raise the fine maxima as well as to formalize day fines.

Despite somewhat higher fine amounts, the Staten Island court's collection rate has remained high. Although not all the data are in as yet, 70 percent of the offenders sentenced to day fines have paid the full amount set at sentencing and another 1.3 percent had paid a substantial proportion of the day fine before the court remitted the balance. (To date, 77 percent of the day-fine dollars levied by the court have been collected.) In an additional 2 percent of the day-fine cases, payments are still being made or the fine has been stayed pending appeal of the conviction.

Finally, 13 percent of the offenders sentenced to day fines have been returned to court for resentencing (generally to community service, "time served," or a jail term averaging eleven days). In all, therefore, 84 percent of the offenders sentenced to day fines have had their sentences enforced by the court, most through payment of the original amount and a few through revocation of the fine and a resentence. Furthermore, to achieve this level of enforcement, there has been relatively little need to resort to the most coercive device available, imprisonment for default (10 percent of the completed cases have been jailed). Enforcement has been unsuccessful to date for 14 percent of the offenders sentenced to day fines for whom arrest warrants are currently outstanding.

The experiences of the Staten Island day-fine project demonstrate that the day fine can be crafted to fit into the sentencing practices and routine operations of an American court; they also indicate that the day fine has some potential advantages over traditional fixed fines. This suggests that broader use of the day fine in American courts might enable the fine sentence to fulfill its potential as a significant—perhaps even central—intermediate penalty.

Day-Fine Projects Launched in Four Jurisdictions
Susan Turner

Four day-fine pilot projects began operation in 1991 and 1992 as part of a nationwide demonstration program funded by the Bureau of Justice Assistance (BJA). The projects build on experience gained in the first American day-fine project conducted in Staten Island, New York, by the Vera Institute of Justice. The jurisdictions selected to participate are Maricopa County, Arizona; Polk County, Iowa; Bridgeport, Connecticut; and Marion, Malheur, Josephine, and Coos Counties in Oregon. BJA selected the Vera Institute of Justice and the Institute for Court Management to provide technical assistance and training to the selected sites. RAND was awarded a grant by the National Institute of Justice to evaluate the demonstration projects.

Day fines, though common in many European countries and recently implemented nationwide in England and Wales, are not widely used in the United States. The first pilot project in Staten Island was judged successful along a number of dimensions and generated substantial additional revenues for the courts. The BJA-sponsored projects are the first major multisite day-fine projects. This article describes the individual projects and sketches evaluation plans.

Central to each jurisdiction's program are two key day-fine concepts. Benchmarks have been established that specify the numbers (or ranges) of penalty units for crimes of different severity. Procedures have been developed to calculate an offender's daily income. The daily income is then multiplied by the number of penalty units to arrive at the fine amount. Contracts are worked out with offenders to specify payment schedules and amounts to be paid, and sanctions are imposed for nonpayment. However, each of the four jurisdictions has adapted the day-fine concept to its own local needs and interests.

MARICOPA COUNTY, ARIZONA

The day-fine program, Financial Assessment Related to Employability (or FARE supervision as it is called), in Maricopa County, Arizona, is administered through the probation department and targets low-risk and low-need felony offenders convicted in superior court who have traditionally received standard probation supervision. FARE is intended to serve as an intermediate sanction between routine probation and summary (unsupervised) probation.

Offenders are eligible for FARE if they have been convicted of a probation-eligible offense; are not in need of formal supervision (e.g., not chronic offenders, prone to violation); do not require treatment, training, or education; and do not owe large amounts of restitution. Eligible offenses are assigned specific penalty units. Offenders are nominated for FARE by probation officers during the presentence investigation process. For eligible offenders, the officer calculates daily income based on information provided by the offender and fills out a day-fine worksheet that specifies the unit value, the number of penalty units, and the resulting fine amount. Final determination to impose the structured fine is made by the judge at sentencing.

FARE supervision is provided by a special FARE probation officer whose primary goal is to collect the financial assessment in as short a period as possible. Modifications can be made to the original assessment amount and payment schedule if, despite a good-faith effort, the offender is unable to pay. Willful nonpayment can result in a term of incarceration in the county jail.

POLK COUNTY, IOWA

The day-fine program in Polk County (Des Moines) became operational in January 1992 and is administered from the county attorney's office. Offenders charged with serious and aggravated misdemeanors (lowest-level misdemeanors are not eligible) are currently targeted by the program, although felony cases are expected to be included later. Eligibility is based mainly on offense type, but offenders with serious prior records or high needs for probation services may be excluded. Eligible offenses are assigned specific penalty units.

Initial screening is performed by assistant county attorneys who determine whether a case is fine-eligible. Financial calculations are made by day-fine staff. The resulting fine amount is determined and provided to the assistant county attorneys. The calculated fine amount is discussed in plea negotiations. Prosecutors recommend the computed fine to the judges, who make the final determination on its imposition.

A day-fine officer oversees the project with the assistance of two project aides. They are responsible for monitoring and enforcing the payments.

BRIDGEPORT, CONNECTICUT

The Bridgeport program began operation in May 1992. Its goals are to make fines more equitable and to increase the use of fines both for offenses currently punished by fines and for offenses not previously fined. The participating court in the demonstration project handles both felonies and misdemeanors; offenses ranging from class B felonies to class C misdemeanors are eligible. Cases can be referred from any stage in court processing.

Unlike Maricopa and Polk Counties, which specify a prescribed number of day-fine units for particular conviction offenses, the Bridgeport program sets out broad ranges of penalty units for each offense. The exact number of fine units for an individual case is generally negotiated during plea bargaining. Financial information is then reviewed by the project day-fine officer, who verifies the offender's income. The officer calculates the fine and recommends it to the court. The final decision to impose a day fine is made by the judge.

Offenders either pay in full at the time of conviction or work with the day-fine officer to prepare an installment plan acceptable to the court. Because of complexities in Connecticut law, offenders who are to make installment payments have their fines imposed and vacated, and their cases continued. Once payments are made in full, the fine is reimposed on the record.

As in the other sites, the day-fine officer is responsible for monitoring and enforcing payments. Offenders who default are rearrested and brought back before the court.

COOS, JOSEPHINE, MALHEUR, AND MARION COUNTIES, OREGON

Four counties are participating in the Oregon day-fine project. The programs in Coos, Josephine, and Malheur counties target presumptive probation felonies and all misdemeanors. Marion County, the largest county, targets only misdemeanors. Penalty units are assigned in 15–30-unit ranges for classes of offense; a presumptive penalty unit is in the center of each range.

The Marion program began in May 1992. Cases are eligible for a day fine after a plea of guilty or no contest in lower court. Before the plea, a unit value worksheet is completed based on information generally provided from the defendant's affidavit of indigency. This worksheet is provided to the judge along with a verbal recommendation by the district attorney concerning the number of penalty units. The judge retains final responsibility for determining the number of penalty units for the offense and the final day-fine amount.

After sentencing, the offender meets with the day-fine officer to complete a contract specifying payment amounts and dates. The officer is responsible for monitoring and enforcing the contract, as well as making revisions to the contract. Delinquent offenders are warned through phone calls and warning letters, culminating in a warrant for arrest for non-payment.

THE RAND EVALUATION

RAND's evaluation is comprehensive and involves process and outcome evaluations and comprehensive case studies of each jurisdiction. The case studies examine program design and implementation, administrative and statutory changes required to implement the programs, staff training, and program costs. The case studies will identify how contextual factors enhance or impede the project's implementation.

The outcome evaluation will examine program effects on sentencing practices, fine payment, collection and enforcement activities, and offenders' criminal behavior. To determine the effects of the day-fine program on sentencing practices generally, the evaluation will compare cohorts of offenders sentenced before and after the implementation of the programs. These analyses will highlight whether fines are used more often, variations in fines imposed, and changes in the use of other types of sentences, including jail and probation as a result of the programs.

More intensive efforts will be devoted to analyzing one-year follow-up outcomes for offenders who received day fines and a matched group of similar offenders who did not receive day fines. Key questions include whether day-fine offenders are more likely to pay their fines; whether probation officers or the court respond differently in terms of enforcement and collection activities; whether day-fine offenders are more or less likely to incur technical violations and arrests than are offenders not subject to such fines; and whether the estimated costs of supervising day-fine offenders are greater than for comparable offenders.

PROGRESS TO DATE

The participating day-fine programs are nearing the end of their initial implementation phases. Data are being collected for both the process and outcome evaluations. Interim results are expected by mid-1993, with complete evaluation results expected in 1994.

England Adopts Unit Fines
David Moxon

A unit-fine scheme—akin to day fines but based on a week's income rather than a day's—took effect in magistrates' courts throughout England and Wales in October 1992. This article looks at the reasons why the idea of unit fines took root, discusses experiments in four courts that convinced policymakers that unit fines could work, and describes the new statutory scheme.

BACKGROUND

Most offenders in England and Wales are dealt with in lower courts called magistrates' courts. These courts deal with all minor offenses, including most motor vehicle cases, and for these a fine is almost always imposed. However, these courts also deal with large numbers of more serious offenses, including theft, burglary, assault, and criminal damage.

During the 1980s the proportion of offenders fined for such offenses fell substantially, and there was an offsetting increase in the use of probation and community service. These sanctions are, for the most part, much more costly and no more effective at deterring people from further offending. Those fined are, if anything, slightly less likely to be convicted of additional offenses after allowing for type of offense and previous convictions.

So why had the fine lost ground? Most likely a rise in unemployment led to more defaults, and hence to more imprisonment for default. Magistrates responded by imposing fewer fines.

Although the proportion imprisoned for default has never exceeded 1.6 percent of those fined, the number doubled in a decade, reaching a peak of around 26,000 in 1982, when fine defaulters represented about a quarter of all prison receptions. Fine defaulters are housed mostly in local prisons, equivalent to American jails, where overcrowding is worst.

Default by nonpayment was clearly a problem that posed a dilemma. How can offenders be fined sums they can afford, without sending the wrong signals as to seriousness of offenses? A large fine invites default. A small fine may be seen as derisory. As long ago as 1970 a parliamentary committee looked at the Swedish day-fine system, but concluded that it would be impractical in Britain. As day fines spread in Europe, however, and as use of the conventional fine declined, discussion about day fines resumed.

THE EXPERIMENTS

Some believed a day-fine scheme impracticable. Particular concerns were that it would be difficult to assess means, and that attempts to match fines closely to income would increase case disposition time and aggravate court delays. To test the day fine's feasibility, the Home Office established four pilot projects and evaluated their effect on court operations, sums imposed, sums collected, and imprisonment for default.

Although the schemes drew on European experience, they were tailored to English and Welsh courts. Other European schemes have based fines on spare daily income. This seemed an unnecessary complication: few people budget, or are paid, on a daily basis, and it is easier to calculate income and expenditure over a longer period. The term *unit fine* was adopted—it embraces day fines as well as fines based on any other period over which income is measured, and weekly spare income was used as the unit.

One goal was to test the feasibility of obtaining means information. A fairly simple form sought details of income, the number of children and adults supported from that income, and any expenditures out of the ordinary. Allowances were fixed according to the number of adults and children in the family. It was felt that detailed investigation of income and expenditure would be inappropriate: what people actually spend on such things as food and clothing does not necessarily reflect what they need to spend, and in any case the need to relate fines to means would have foundered if it had added greatly to the complexity of handling cases.

THE KEY FINDINGS

1. The consensus among magistrates and court staff at all the courts involved in the experiments was that unit fines were an improvement on the previous system, and all continued to use them after the six-month experiments ended.

2. Using a simple form, courts obtained sufficient means information without undue difficulty and without increasing the time taken to process cases.

3. At all the participating courts, the poorest offenders were fined less; at one court, where the norm was set at a higher level, the better-off paid more.

4. A small supplementary survey of people paying at the maximum rate at one court indicated that many could have afforded to pay more than the local norm.

5. Disparities between courts in fines imposed on poorer offenders were significantly reduced.

6. Fines were paid more quickly. At all the courts, significantly higher proportions of fines were paid in full within six or twelve months. The average time taken to complete payment fell by one quarter at three of the courts; there was no

change at the fourth despite an increase in average amounts imposed.

7. The proportion of those fined who were imprisoned for default fell by about one quarter.

The experiments did not provide a full test of a comprehensive day-fine system. This is because the Court of Appeal had ruled that fines can be reduced for those of limited means, but cannot be increased for the wealthy. Only a change in legislation would have permitted this, and it would have been difficult to justify imposing much larger fines on individuals at selected courts as part of an experiment. Nevertheless, the results suggested that unit fines would be practicable, and the necessary legislation—which enables courts to impose larger fines on the affluent—is now in place.

IMPLEMENTATION

Legislation introducing unit fines nationally took effect in October 1992. To avoid criticisms that some fines could be so small as to appear insignificant, and as such offer no deterrent, the minimum unit value is £4, and guidelines suggest that there may sometimes be a need to impose a minimum sum to avoid the offender showing a "profit." An example is driving without insurance, where the fine could cost an offender much less than the premium. To avoid very large fines being imposed for minor offenses, an upper limit of £100 per unit will apply. The past practice of limiting payment to twelve months will remain, and the maximum fine will thus be £5,000.

Guidance is being offered to courts with the aim of promoting consistency in the way fines are calculated. First, the Magistrates' Association is issuing recommendations to help in determining the number of units appropriate for a given type of offense. (The figure is no more than a starting point, to be modified according to the circumstances of the individual case.) Second, the Home Office is issuing guidance as to how courts should set the amount of each unit. Advice covers such matters as the items courts should take into account when calculating allowances to be set against income, the items to be covered by the means forms, arrangements for the forms' distribution and completion, and the way fines are to be announced in court.

The excess of income over expenditure based on allowances will be used to calculate the fine. However, an important refinement was made following consultation with the courts. If all income was taken to pay the fine once the basic threshold was passed, up to the £100 maximum, it was felt this would bite too harshly on middle-income offenders. People's life-styles are geared to income, and most people on average or above-average incomes would find it difficult to adjust their expenditures in the short term to the level of the poorest. For example, housing and transportation costs often cannot be quickly adjusted. Also, in taking every additional pound, the £100 limit could in some cases be reached on comparatively modest incomes, and a more progressive scale was preferred. The rules, therefore, provide that the amount of each unit should be fixed by taking one third of the available income above the basic level. Where the spare income is less than £4, this minimum will still apply, although there would be scope for a later reduction if the court decided that even the minimum was beyond the means of the offender. The poorest offenders, dependent on state benefit, could in some cases have fines paid through deductions. This is an extension of arrangements that already apply to the payment of certain other obligations such as for fuel and housing. As so many of those imprisoned for default are living on state benefits, this could greatly reduce the number of defaulters sent to prison.

Quite apart from the findings from the pilot studies, crucial lessons were learned from the experience as a whole. The first was the importance of having direct practical experience to draw on in framing legislation and planning its implementation. The second was the importance of consultation with those who would operate the new schemes. If practitioners in the courts can be convinced of the advantages of the scheme, and their reservations are taken into account, any scheme will be much more likely to succeed. The final stage will be for the Home Office to monitor the way the new provisions work. If necessary, adjustments will be made to ensure that arrangements work as smoothly and consistently as possible.

England Abandons Unit Fines
David Moxon

After only seven months, the English government abandoned its unit-fine initiative and repealed the enabling legislation. For the present, at least, the effort to incorporate means-based fines akin to day fines into the system of penal sanctions is at an end. A number of problems contributed to the government's decision, not the least being extensive media accounts of bizarrely harsh fines for trivial crimes, the most celebrated a littering fine of £1,200 for tossing a potato chip bag on the ground. This article tells the story of England's brief and troubled experience with unit fines.

BACKGROUND

In the June 1992 edition of *Overcrowded Times* I wrote about the success of pilot projects designed to test the feasibility of unit fines—similar to day fines but based on a week's income rather than a day's. The basic principle is that the number of units imposed for an offense is determined by the seriousness of the offense, and the amount of each unit is determined by the offender's weekly disposable income—the income left over after allowing for basic expenditures.

The pilot projects were carried out in magistrates' courts, which have full jurisdiction over minor crimes and concurrent jurisdiction with higher courts over some more serious crimes. The pilot projects had the support of the magistrates and court staff where they had been introduced, not least because they were felt to have been fairer than the old system; a result was greater consistency between courts when fining people of similar means than had been the case previously. The scheme made enforcement easier, with fines paid more quickly and with less imprisonment for default. It was hoped that the ability to match fines to offenders' circumstances in a more systematic way would help to reverse the long-term decline in the use of the fine.

Encouraged by the evaluation research, the government introduced legislation that gave statutory force to unit fines with effect from October 1992. There were important differences between the national scheme and the pilot schemes. Perhaps the most crucial was that, when the pilots were conducted, fines could be reduced for lack of means but could not be increased for the better-off. Pilot project courts set the range for units of disposable income locally so that well-off offenders paid roughly the same fines as they would have under the previous system. In practice, the maximum sum for each unit ranged from £10 sterling to £20 (at current exchange rates, $15 to $30), reflecting perceived differences in average local income. A nominal minimum unit value was set at £3, but in some courts this was reduced still further for the very poorest offenders.

By contrast, under the unit-fine legislation, the range of unit values widened to £4 and £100. As a result, fines could be much larger, particularly as the maximum fine that magistrates have authority to impose was raised from £2,000 to £5,000. Means assessment therefore assumed much greater importance than in the pilot schemes, particularly as all types of offense were included.

ASSESSING MEANS

Each court set local allowances based on family composition and estimates of typical local housing costs. The form was kept simple since it was felt that a complicated form was less likely to be filled in, and a detailed breakdown of expenditure would be largely irrelevant, though allowance could be made for exceptional obligations. The unit value was assessed as one-third of the residual income after taking account of allowances. However, if there were few allowances to set against income the maximum £100 unit value could be reached on quite modest incomes. It was felt by many magistrates that the scheme failed to acknowledge that, as income rises, so do financial commitments that cannot easily be reduced in the short term. Before the scheme was scrapped, many of those involved had urged changes that would have permitted a slower increase in fines as incomes rose, for example, by defining the unit value as a proportion of total income.

The increase in maximum fines did, of course, make it much more important to have good means information in every case. All defendants were sent a means form, but there was no legal obligation for them to complete it in advance of the case, partly because it was felt that it would be wrong to impose such a requirement on people who might at that stage be protesting their innocence. If the offender was in court he or she could be asked to complete a form while waiting for the case to be heard, or asked questions in court. However, in minor (and particularly minor motor vehicle) cases, offenders commonly pleaded guilty by mail. If the means form was not returned with the guilty plea, the court then either had to adjourn the case for means information to be supplied or to make a judgment based on little or no information.

If the court had some information—for example, if it was known that the offender was unemployed or alternatively what the offender's job was—a reasonable estimate could often be made. However, if there was no information, after the offender had been given the opportunity of providing it, what should the court do? Some fell back on an arbitrary figure of, say, £20, which they felt would be fairly realistic in the general run of cases and would avoid further delay or complication. Others took the view that this approach was unjust, in that someone who was relatively well off and took the trouble to tell the court would be fined more severely than someone who simply kept quiet about his means. The maximum unit value of £100 was then likely to be imposed, leaving it to the offender to challenge this assessment later on if he felt it was excessive.

SCOPE OF UNIT FINES

In contrast to other jurisdictions that have adopted day fines, the unit-fine system covered all offenses that reached magistrates' courts (though the scheme did not apply in the higher courts). It was felt that drawing a distinction between offenses liable to unit fines and those that were not would inevitably be somewhat arbitrary, and that a common system for all offenses would be simpler to administer. Calculating the fine would otherwise be especially awkward when a mix of offenses was dealt with on the same occasion. Some doubts were expressed, however, over whether the complication of a means inquiry was appropriate for very trivial matters. Minor motor-vehicle offenses posed special difficulties because they are usually dealt with by means of fixed penalties but can go to court for reasons that have nothing to do with seriousness. To take one example, by law an American serviceman stationed in England cannot be dealt with by way of fixed penalty for a driving offense and so must go to court even on a very minor matter. This could result in a fine of several hundred pounds instead of the £36 fixed penalty that most other people would pay. The potential anomaly was recognized insofar as the legislation provided for fines to be increased to the level of the fixed penalty so that the poorest offenders would not have an incentive to take trivial cases to court, but there was no corresponding power to reduce the fine to avoid unfairness.

In practice, some courts took the view—with the approval of other local criminal-justice agencies—that where a fixed penalty would have been appropriate but could not be applied for technical reasons the unit-fine provisions should be overridden. This could be done by arbitrarily reducing the number of units or fixing the unit sum at a low level, or by giving a discharge but requiring the offender to pay costs of an amount similar to the fixed penalty.

PROBLEM CASES

The foreseeable result of raising the maximum unit value to £100, of adopting the maximum in the absence of means information, and of including all offenses in the scheme was that large fines were sometimes imposed for very minor offenses. Because such cases and the publicity they attracted contributed strongly to the scheme's downfall, it is instructive to look at a couple of the numerous examples that caught the headlines. In the first, magistrates fined a man £500 for illegal parking after his car broke down on a road where parking was prohibited. He had exercised his right to take the case to court, rather than pay the fixed penalty by mail, because he thought he had a legitimate defense. A flawed means assessment resulted in the unit rate being set at the £100 maximum, yielding a fine that according to press reports amounted to more than twice the value of the vehicle. On appeal, the Crown Court (quite sensibly) reduced the fine to the level of a fixed penalty.

Cases of this sort highlighted two anomalies. First, a unit fine could be totally disproportionate to the fixed penalty that would normally apply, making it very difficult for anyone who felt he had a defense to challenge it. (Automobile clubs were quick to advise their members to pay up, even if they thought they were innocent, rather than risk losing in court.) Second, magistrates' authority and the credibility of unit fines were undermined by the fact that the unit-fine principle was applicable only in magistrates' courts but not in the higher Crown Court; on appeal, it was up to the individual judge. In the particular instance of the parking fine, the magistrate's view of the seriousness of the offense—awarding 5 units on a scale of 1 to 10—was out of step with the public and media perception of the offense. So what was widely perceived as an unjust decision regarding the nature and seriousness of the alleged offense was unfairly—but understandably—blamed on the unit-fine system. In this way, factors outside the unit-fine scheme contributed to its downfall.

In the second example, a man was fined £1,200 for throwing a potato chip bag onto the ground instead of placing it in a nearby litter bin. The penalty in terms of the number of units was higher than usual in such cases because the offender refused to pick the litter up and was cheeky to the policeman who witnessed the incident. The unit value was fixed at £100 because the offender failed to provide any means information. However, later on evidence was received that he was unemployed, and the fine was reduced to the minimum level for 12 units, i.e., £48. The system worked effectively and fairly, but not before a great deal of publicity had been given in the national press to the curiosity that an unemployed man had been fined £1,200 for carelessly discarding a potato chip bag.

THE LESSONS

The English experience clearly has implications for any jurisdiction contemplating the introduction of day or unit fines, bearing in mind that acceptance by both the public and sentencers is crucial to success.

If the unit values span too wide a range, the amount of the fine is influenced much more by assessment of means than by offense seriousness. Sentencers are often uneasy at the contrast between small fines for relatively serious matters and large fines for minor offenses. This was a major issue in England and Wales, although it does not appear to have troubled sentencers in other jurisdictions that use day fines, even when much higher maxima are often available. One reason may be that minor offenses, of the sort that caused some of the most damaging criticism, are not normally included in day-fine schemes.

Quite apart from the problem of large fines for minor offenses, inclusion of all offenses can create anomalies when compared with any fixed penalty system (which by definition takes no account of means). The kinds of examples cited above raise the question of whether trivial incidents justify an investigation into income and expenses, with all the difficulties that arise when means information is not forthcoming. If the system is confined to more serious matters, the offender will usually be in court, and questions about means can be raised if no form has been provided.

It is important that those operating the scheme understand and accept both its principles and its practical implications. Support for the principles was in many cases undermined because of perceived injustices in certain types of cases. The need to ensure that the principles are applied consistently should not result in such rigid rules and loss of discretion that sentencers are faced with either breaking the rules or imposing sentences that they feel are unfair. (A few magistrates were so worried by the decisions they felt the legislation was obliging them to take that they resigned.)

If fines are subject to review on appeal, the appellate judges should be subject to the criteria that applied in the lower court that set the original fine, although clearly both the number of units and the amount of each unit are proper matters for review by the appellate court.

During the seven months in which the unit-fine scheme was in operation, these points received a good deal of attention and consideration, and there were signs of a consensus developing in some quarters as to how to resolve them. However, unit fines came under such heavy and sustained attack from large sections of the media—and often from magistrates—that government ministers felt it better to scrap what was felt to be too mechanistic and rigid a scheme. What has replaced it does not take England and Wales back to the preexisting situation; courts are now able to increase fines for the better-off and to reduce them for the poor. The legislation also makes it clear that means are still relevant when setting fines, and courts can evolve whatever measures they think most appropriate for taking means into account. It will be interesting to see whether the experience of relating fines to means in a systematic way will have a lasting impact on the way fines are set.

Fines Reduce Use of Prison Sentences in Germany
Thomas Weigend

Between 1968 and 1989, the former West Germany greatly reduced the proportion of convicted offenders sentenced to prison. In 1968, roughly a quarter of convicted offenders were sentenced to imprisonment. Two years later, the size of that group had dropped from 136,000 to 42,000, and the percentage of convicted offenders who were imprisoned had fallen from 24 percent to 7 percent. In 1989 (the latest year for which data are available), only 33,000 persons, less than 6 percent of adults convicted in West Germany, were sent directly to prison.

It is important for North American readers to understand that these figures include all persons sentenced to incarceration—the equivalent in the United States of sentenced jail inmates plus prison inmates. This article tells the story of how and why West Germany has steadily reduced its reliance on prisons.

The remarkable decline in prison use is due to a determined assault on use of short-term imprisonment. At the turn of the century, more than 50 percent of offenders received prison sentences of three months' duration or less. Legislation passed in 1921 obliged the courts to impose fines instead of short prison terms whenever the purpose of punishment could as well be achieved by a fine. Even so, the portion of short prison sentences among all prison sentences remained high; 83 percent of offenders sentenced to imprisonment in 1968 received sentences of six months or less. By that time, the German legislature had embraced the idea that short-term imprisonment does more harm than good: it disrupts the offender's ties with his family, job, and friends, introduces him into the prison subculture, and stigmatizes him for the rest of his life, but does not allow sufficient time for promising rehabilitative measures. Moreover, the data on the deterrent effectiveness of short-term imprisonment were inconclusive at best.

As a consequence, the German legislature in 1970 enacted section 47, sub. 1 of the Penal Code: "The court shall impose imprisonment below six months only if special circumstances concerning the offense or the offender's personality make the imposition of a prison sentence indispensable for reforming the offender or for defending the legal order." That amendment meant, in effect, that prison sentences below six months could be imposed only under exceptional circumstances for purposes of rehabilitation or general prevention. The number of such sentences dropped dramatically from 184,000 (1968) to 56,000 (1970); after some ups and downs, that figure reached a low of 48,000 in 1989 (and many of these were suspended).

At the same time, the German legislature extended the possibility of suspending short-term prison sentences (suspension being the German equivalent of probation). According to section 56 of the Penal Code, the court shall suspend the execution of prison sentences of up to one year whenever the offender can be expected to refrain from further offenses without a prison experience. German law expressly prohibits split sentences: prison sentences can only be suspended or executed in full (except for the possibility of parole, which exists after the offender has served one half of his term). Sentences of more than two years' imprisonment cannot be suspended.

When the court suspends a prison sentence, it determines a probationary period of two to five years; suspension can be revoked (and the sentence executed) if the offender commits another crime during that period. The court can combine suspension with various conditions and restrictions, including the duty to make restitution to the victim or to pay a sum of money to the state or to a charitable organization, to avoid the company of certain individuals, and to report regularly to the court or to the police. The offender can also be assigned to a probation officer.

German courts have made use of the suspension option with consistently increasing frequency. In 1968, the year before the reform, only 36 percent of prison sentences were suspended. By 1979, that portion had climbed to 65 percent, and it has not significantly changed since then (1989—67 percent). Prison sentences of six months or less have been suspended even more liberally (1989—77 percent). Revocations of suspension have diminished despite the more generous use of suspension. Whereas 46 percent of suspensions were revoked in 1986, less than a third (29 percent) were revoked in 1989.

For minor offenses, German law since 1975 offers an additional option of informal sanctioning. According to section 153a of the Code of Criminal Procedure, either the public prosecutor or the court can "invite" a suspect to pay a sum of money to the state, the victim, or a charitable organization in exchange for dismissal of the criminal prosecution. The theory of this quasi-sanction is that the suspect, by making the payment, eliminates the public interest in prosecuting the minor offense. The payment neither requires a formal admission of guilt nor implies a criminal conviction, but the (presumed) offender must pay an amount of money roughly equivalent to the fine that might be imposed if he were convicted. The use of this procedural option has greatly increased since its inception; prosecutors and courts employ it not only in petty cases but also for sanctioning fairly serious, especially economic, offenses without trial. Taking the quasi-sanction of section 153a into account, the distribution of criminal sanctions in Germany before and after the reforms of 1970 and 1975 is shown in figure 1.

The de-emphasis of nonsuspended short prison sentences and the introduction of conditional dismissal produced a marked shift from custodial sentences (which, even in 1968,

Part I Monetary Penalties

Figure 1: Criminal Sanctions, 1968 and 1989

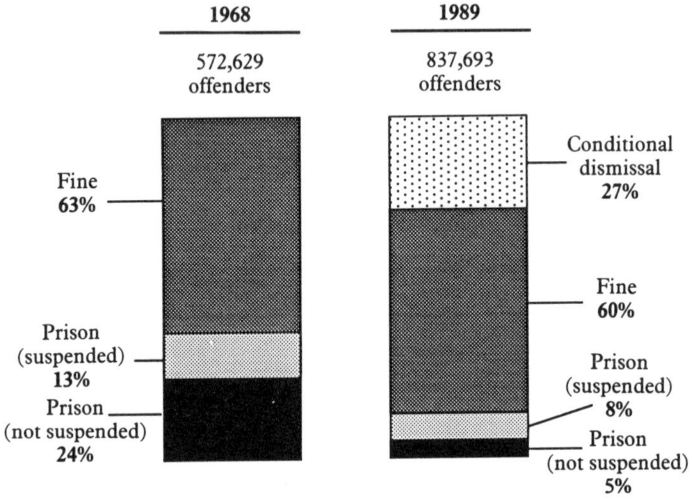

Sources: Statistisches Bundesamt, Fachserie A., Reihe 9: Rechtspflege 1968, p. 120; Statistisches Bundesamt, Fachserie 10, Reihe 3: Strafverfolgung 1989, p. 42; Statistisches Bundesamt, Staatsanwaltschaften 1989, p. 14.

had a comparatively low incidence) to monetary sanctions. One might expect this shift to have led to a proportional depletion of German prisons. Curiously, that has failed to occur. Figure 2 shows the numbers of persons (excluding pretrial detainees) held in German prisons on March 31 of selected years.

Although the reform of 1970 brought about an immediate sharp reduction of the prison population, by 1984 the number of prisoners had surpassed the high point of 1968. Since that time there has been a slow but steady decline.

Cynics might argue that the rise in the number of prisoners in spite of the decline of imprisonment rates demonstrates that available prison space will always be filled. Yet there are rational explanations for this development. First, the overall number of convicted offenders has increased, though not dramatically, from 573,000 (1968) to 609,000 (1989). More

46

Figure 2: Number of Persons Held in German Prisons, 1968–1989 (excluding pretrial detainees)

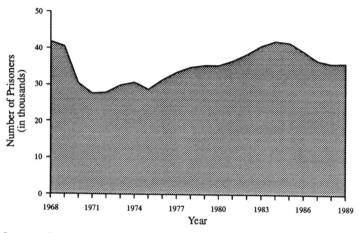

Sources: Statistisches Bundesamt, Fachserie A, Reihe 9: Rechtspflege 1968, 1971, 1973; Statistisches Bundesamt, Fachserie 10, Reihe 1: Ausgewahlte Zählen für die Rechtspflege 1984, 1988, 1989.

important, those who receive nonsuspended prison sentences tend to receive longer sentences than before: within fifteen years, the share of lengthy sentences (two to fifteen years) among all nonsuspended prison sentences increased from 9 percent (1974) to 15 percent. This change may be due to the increase in drug-related offenses, which tend to draw heavy sentences.

Moreover, the initial imposition of a noncustodial sentence does not necessarily mean that the offender can avoid prison, since about one third of suspended sentences are revoked (usually due to the commission of a new offense). Offenders who receive fines can be sent to prison for nonpayment. Under German law, nonpayment can transform a fine into a prison term; the state need not show that the offender willfully refused to pay although he had the means to do so (section 43, Penal Code). Although only 6–7 percent of fined offenders eventually serve a prison term because of nonpayment, this group, due to the large absolute numbers involved, imposes a heavy burden on the corrections system: each year approximately 30,000 such persons enter prison.

In recent years, the German states have increasingly attempted to reduce that number by offering destitute offenders an alternative to prison. They can enter community service programs and thereby work off the fine instead of "sitting it off." These programs, though reaching only a limited number of offenders, have been described as fairly successful, especially when they are adequately staffed and organized.

Has the reduced emphasis on imprisonment in the German sentencing system led to an avalanche of new crime? Superficially, the figures seem to support that notion, as seen in figure 3.

The absolute as well as the relative incidence of crime known to the police has roughly doubled within the twenty years since the reform of sentencing law. However, several considerations make the existence of a causal link between the two developments most unlikely. A closer look at the statistics reveals that the fairly abrupt 1970 change in sentencing practice is not reflected in the steadily rising curve of the crime

Figure 3: Offenses Known to Police, 1968–1989 (excluding traffic offenses)

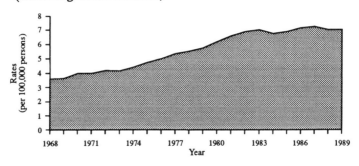

Source: Bundeskriminalamt, Polizeiliche Kriminalstatistik 1989, 1990, p. 11.

rate; its increase precedes 1968. However, there is no change in sentencing practice to explain the leveling off of the crime rate after 1983. Moreover, the police statistics tell us very little about actual changes in the occurrence of crime since they cannot provide knowledge of offenses not detected, not reported, or not recorded by the police. Finally, common criminological wisdom has it that crime rates are influenced by demographic, economic, and social factors to an overwhelmingly greater extent than by sentencing styles. (If it were otherwise, the United States should have a minuscule crime problem compared to, say, the Netherlands or Japan.)

It is more interesting to look at the relationship between crime and criminal justice from the opposite side. What effect does the (perceived) increase of the crime problem have on sentencing? As we have seen, official sentencing policy in Germany has responded in an anticyclical fashion by discouraging the imposition of prison sentences in the face of a growing crime rate. The statistics cited above have demonstrated three features, which can possibly be interpreted as effects of the legislature's remarkable policy decision: the courts have greatly reduced the proportion of nonsuspended prison sentences; the overall number of convicted persons has remained stable; and the number of prisoners has fluctuated and has now returned to the level of the 1960s.

German policies, and the faithful implementation of their directives by prosecutors and courts, have led to a "cushioning" of the crime wave of the 1970s. A greater percentage of offenses than before were resolved without conviction, and potential overcrowding of prisons was avoided by increased use of fines and suspended sentences. The crime wave ebbed after 1983, independent of any action or inaction on the part of criminal justice policymakers. It can only be hoped that they keep as cool today as they did in the 1960s, even in view of the problems associated with reunification and with the currently publicized arrival of "organized crime" in Germany.

In Germany, Fines Often Imposed in Lieu of Prosecution

Thomas Weigend

German law gives misdemeanor offenders the option of avoiding a criminal trial and conviction by paying a sum of money to the victim, a charitable organization, or the state. This option is provided by section 153a of the German Code of Criminal Procedure, in force since 1975. It was designed as a diversionary measure that benefits the criminal-justice system as well as the accused: the state imposes a sanction without having to conduct a trial, and the offender avoids a criminal record. If the offender pays the required amount, criminal proceedings are dismissed, and no lasting record is made of the incident.

At the time of its introduction, section 153a was criticized as permitting unseemly bartering and bargaining over criminal justice. Prosecutors, courts, and defendants have welcomed the possibility of dismissing criminal charges in exchange for certain payments, and section 153a has turned out to be a successful way of dealing with less serious crime without imprisonment or probation.

THE LEGAL CONTEXT

The concept of dismissing criminal cases in response to the defendant's efforts to make good is alien to traditional principles of the German criminal process. In earlier times, informal practices of that sort were generally regarded as plain violations of the prosecutor's duty to bring charges in every case with sufficient evidence for conviction. However, strict application of the ancient principle of mandatory prosecution has in recent years been limited to the most serious crimes (felonies punishable by a minimum of one year's imprisonment). With respect to lesser offenses, the public prosecutor has been given greater leeway to decide whether prosecuting convictable offenders would be in the public interest.

Section 153a takes that development one step further. It is based on the theory that the offender can satisfy the public interest in prosecution by making a payment or by taking other actions (e.g., doing community work) for the public good. By compensating the victim or by giving to charity, the defendant implicitly acknowledges his responsibility for the offense and at the same time demonstrates his willingness to act in a socially commendable way, thus obviating the need to impose punishment. Although such payments, particularly when made to the state, very much resemble criminal fines, the statute carefully avoids any such designation. Unilaterally imposing a fine as a criminal sanction before conviction would clearly violate the presumption of innocence and would also infringe upon the German judiciary's constitutional prerogative to impose criminal punishment. For these reasons, the imposition of payments under section 153a requires the prior consent of the defendant and can thus be treated as voluntary.

THE PROCESS

Dismissal of charges under section 153a ("conditional dismissal") requires a fairly complicated procedure, but German practice keeps the law's encumbrances to a minimum. The initiative for conditional dismissal can be taken by the prosecution or the defense. Generally, the prosecutor proposes dismissal to the defendant and suggests the amount to be paid. If the defendant has a lawyer, the attorney may approach the prosecutor and propose a conditional dismissal. In either case, the appropriate amount of payment can be subject to bargaining. Although, according to section 153a, the prosecutor should contemplate a resolution only when he or she is convinced of the defendant's guilt, uncertainties about trial outcomes may be a factor in the discussion between the parties, as the defendant will weigh acquittal chances against the financial sacrifices section 153a demands. Section 153a does not require the defendant to confess his guilt but only to consent to the proposed disposition—which undoubtedly makes this option attractive to defendants with a reputation to uphold.

If the charges are serious, the prosecutor must present the proposed settlement to the judge for approval (which is seldom withheld). When the defendant submits proof that he has made the required payment or fulfilled the work assignment, the prosecutor dismisses the case. It can be reopened only if new evidence indicates that the offense was not a mere misdemeanor but a felony. A dismissed case is not entered into the defendant's criminal record.

Conditional dismissal can also occur after indictment. Before or after the beginning of the trial, the court can dismiss a case under the same conditions as the prosecutor could before trial. Such resolution can be initiated by the court or by either party; in any event, the consent of both prosecutor and defendant is required.

The victim of the offense has no right to be consulted before dismissal or to appeal against that decision.

SCOPE OF APPLICATION

In 1989, conditional dismissal was applied in 240,855 (West) German cases. Seventy-two percent of dismissals occurred pretrial; the rest were court dismissals. Money payments are typically ordered for traffic offenses, shoplifting, and other petty property offenses. However, neither in theory nor in practice has application of section 153a been limited to nonserious crime. Under German law, aggravated assault, fraud, extortion, and most economic and environmental offenses are classified as misdemeanors and thus are eligible for conditional dismissal. Although section 153a was originally limited to instances of minor blameworthiness, prosecutors have been known to dismiss fairly serious white-collar offenses in exchange for payments of 100,000 German marks (approximately $60,000) and more. From March 1, 1993, conditional dismissal is possible in all misdemeanor cases unless the defendant's blameworthiness is so great as to preclude a disposition without trial. Section 153a has also been used as a compromise solution when conviction appeared doubtful because of evidentiary or legal weaknesses of the prosecution's case.

From the criminal justice system's perspective, section 153a's main virtue is to make trials unnecessary or to avoid the need for judges to issue reasoned judgments subject to appeal. Although frequency of its use differs somewhat among judicial districts, one can say that conditional dismissal has become an important tool of prosecutorial decision-making. As table 1 indicates, (West) German prosecutors in 1989 disposed of 6.2 percent of cases under section 153a.

Although 6.2 percent of all dispositions may not seem a large number, conditional dismissals do represent a significant share of those cases that merit prosecution and conviction. But for the existence of the section 153a option, West German prosecutors would have had to file 16 percent more indictments in 1989 than they did. At the trial stage, conditional dismissals under section 153a represented 10 percent of all disposals in criminal courts in 1989 (excluding penal orders that are only routinely "rubberstamped" by the judge).

Section 153a lists five possible beneficiaries of the defendant's efforts—the victim, charitable organizations, the state,

Table 1: Number of cases—1989 (with known offenders): 2,803,379

Disposition:	
Indictment (including penal order)	33.4%
Dismissal for lack of evidence	28.4
Dismissal for insignificance	23.4
Dismissal under section 153a	6.2
Other (including referral to other prosecutor's office)	8.6

Source: Statistisches Bundesamt Wiesbaden, Staatsanwaltschaften 1989, 1991, p. 16.

the community (as the beneficiary of a community service assignment), and the defendant's dependents (to whom the defendant can be ordered to pay alimony). Only payments to the state and to charitable organizations are of any statistical significance, however. Ninety-eight percent of adult offenders in 1989 were ordered to make payments to one or the other, with a slight majority in favor of the state treasury. There is no plausible reason for the virtual exclusion of victim compensation from the section 153a payments, except that supervising payments to the victim may require a slightly greater effort by the prosecutorial bureaucracy.

POLICY ISSUES

Section 153a has, by and large, been a successful innovation. Long-term analyses of prosecutorial and judicial behavior have shown that conditional dismissals have not increased the overall number of criminal sanctions but have largely replaced convictions (rather than straight dismissals). The success of section 153a provides at least part of the explanation for Germany's progress in restricting the use of imprisonment.

Some German authors' objections to the very concept of conditional dismissal reflect concerns based on special features of German law. Some critics fear that section 153a improperly broadens the scope of prosecutorial discretion, and others regard haggling over the price of dismissal as unseemly. Neither concern should bother Americans, who have long accepted the existence of unlimited prosecutorial discretion and of widespread sentence bargaining.

One critical issue, however, transcends the limits of legal systems: the defendant's consent to the prosecutor's disposition is voluntary only in theory. Everyone concerned understands that, given the vagaries of a criminal trial and the resulting psychological strain, the prosecutor's offer to dismiss in exchange for a payment is sometimes an offer too good to refuse even for innocent or otherwise nonconvictable defendants. Voluntariness is, of course, an issue of lesser importance here than in regular plea bargaining, because the defendant's record remains untarnished and the presumption of innocence remains intact. But the price of avoiding trial should not become too high. While payments of a few hundred marks (or dollars) may be acceptable even when consent is somewhat less than voluntary, it is doubtful whether section 153a–type procedures ought to be applied when large sums of money are at stake. In cases of serious economic crime, dismissing charges in exchange for large payments not only reeks of class-biased justice but also burdens defendants with choices they should not have to make. Properly limited to minor offenses, however, conditional dismissal is a sensible solution with obvious advantages for all concerned.

Restitution and Mediation

Mediating Conflict Among Victims and Offenders
Mark S. Umbreit

Our nation's response to crime and victimization is deeply rooted in the principles of "retributive justice." The focus of the criminal-justice system is upon the state as the victim, with the individual victim often being placed in a passive and peripheral role. The character of criminal behavior as conflict between people is minimized.

There is increasing national interest in a different conception of justice—"restorative justice"—that views crime as a violation of one person by another, rather than merely as an offense against the state. Dialogue and negotiation are preferred to adversary processes, with a focus on problem-solving for the future.

Restorative justice principles place the victim and offender in active and interpersonal problem-solving roles. From this perspective, severe punishment of offenders is less important than empowering victims in their search for resolution, impressing upon offenders the human consequences of their behavior and promoting restitution to victims.

Victim-offender mediation and reconciliation programs are now in operation or development in more than 100 jurisdictions in the United States, 30 in Canada, 25 in Germany, 17 in England, and a handful in Italy. Throughout North America and Europe, crime victims are meeting with their offenders, talking about the crime, expressing their concerns, and negotiating restitution.

Crime victims often feel powerless and vulnerable. Some feel twice victimized, first by the criminal and then by a criminal-justice system that lacks the time to address their needs. Many victims become angry at the entire criminal-justice process.

Offenders are rarely confronted with the human dimensions of their criminal behavior—that victims are real people, not just faceless objects without feelings. Nor are offenders often given the opportunity to make personal amends to the people they victimized.

Victim-offender mediation and reconciliation programs give the victim a stake in the criminal-justice process and provide a conflict resolution process that is perceived as fair by both parties. After discussing the crime and expressing their concerns, victims and offenders negotiate a restitution agreement consisting of payment of money or work for the victim's choice of a charity. Some victims want their offender to do odd jobs for them rather than pay cash restitution.

Most victim-offender mediation programs are sponsored by private organizations working closely with the courts. But increasingly, public agencies are sponsoring their own programs.

The mediation process begins when juvenile or adult offenders (most often convicted of such crimes as theft and burglary) are referred by the court. In some programs, offenders are diverted from further court processing if the mediation is successful.

Each case is assigned to a mediator who meets separately with the offender and the victim before the mediation session is scheduled. The mediator listens to each story, explains the program, and encourages their participation. Usually mediators meet first with the offender.

Only after the initial separate contacts and expressions of willingness by both parties to proceed does the mediator schedule a face-to-face meeting. The meeting begins with the mediator explaining his or her role, identifying the agenda, and stating any communication ground rules.

The first part of the meeting focuses on facts and feelings. Victims can express their feelings directly to the person who violated them, and receive answers to such questions as "Why me?" and "How did you get into our house?" and "Were you stalking us and planning on coming back?" Victims are often relieved to see that the offender bears little resemblance to the frightening character they may have imagined.

Offenders are put in the very uncomfortable position of having to face the person they violated. They are given the equally rare opportunity to express remorse in a very personal fashion. Through open discussion of their feelings, both victim and offender can deal with each other as people, often from the same neighborhood, rather than as stereotypes and objects.

The second part of the meeting focuses on victims' losses and possible mutually acceptable restitution agreements as a tangible outcome of conflict resolution and a focal point for accountability. If victim and offender are unable to agree on restitution, the case is referred back to the referral source (often the sentencing judge), with a good likelihood that the offender will be placed in a different program.

Mediators do not impose a restitution settlement. However, in more than 95 percent of all meetings in many programs, written restitution agreements have been negotiated and signed by meeting's end.

Although certainly not meant for all victims and offenders, mediation provides an opportunity for reducing some victims' anger, frustration, and fear; offenders can be held accountable and make amends; victims can receive compensation; and some offenders can be diverted from incarceration.

Research on victim-offender reconciliation programs in Minnesota and Indiana found that both victims and offenders benefit from a more humanizing experience. Victim-offender mediation results in very high levels of participant satisfaction and perceptions of fairness. Mediating victim-offender conflict is the most vivid expression of the principles of restorative justice within the complexities of our nation's criminal-justice systems.

The Effects of Victim-Offender Mediation

Mark S. Umbreit

Victim-offender mediation is offered in a growing number of communities throughout North America and Europe. Although only a handful of programs existed in North America in the late 1970s, there are now more than 120 in the United States and 26 in Canada. Programs operate both before and after adjudication, with both adults and juveniles. Victim-offender mediation is growing more rapidly in Europe, where it began in the mid-1980s.

A recent evaluation of programs in juvenile courts in four sites—Albuquerque, New Mexico; Minneapolis-St. Paul, Minnesota; Oakland, California; and Austin, Texas—showed that victims who participated were satisfied with the programs and less fearful that they would again be crime victims. Participating offenders were also highly satisfied with the programs and likelier than nonparticipants to make restitution payments.

The evaluation was initiated by Minnesota Citizens Council Mediation Services in Minneapolis, with support from a grant from the State Justice Institute in Alexandria, Virginia. Issues investigated related to the mediation process and outcomes, client satisfaction, perceptions of fairness, cost implications, restitution completion, and recidivism.

MEDIATION ELEMENTS

The process of allowing crime victims to meet face-to-face with their offenders in the presence of a trained mediator generally consists of four phases: case intake from referral sources; preparation for mediation, during which the mediator meets separately with the offender and the victim; the mediation session, which consists of a discussion of what occurred and how people felt about it, followed by negotiation of a restitution agreement; and follow-up activities such as monitoring payment of restitution. Victims can get answers to lingering questions and let the offender know how the crime affected them. Offenders learn the real human impact of their behavior and can take direct responsibility for making things right with their victims. The victim has direct input into holding the offender accountable.

SITES

Taken together, 3,142 cases involving juvenile offenders and their victims were referred to the four mediation programs studied during 1990 and 1991. Eighty-three percent involved property crimes and 17 percent crimes of violence. Nearly all were referred by juvenile courts and probation staff. A small number were referred by prosecuting attorneys or police.

Albuquerque. The Victim Offender Mediation Program in Albuquerque was initiated in 1987 as a component of the New Mexico Center for Dispute Resolution. It is co-sponsored by the local juvenile probation department of the state youth authority. In addition to victim-offender mediation, the center operates a parent-child mediation program, a school mediation program, and a mediation program for youth in correctional facilities. During 1990 and 1991, it had a caseload of 591. The program serves a population of about 450,000, including large Hispanic and Native American communities.

Minneapolis-St. Paul. The Center for Victim Offender Mediation in Minneapolis was established by the Minnesota Citizens Council on Crime and Justice in 1985. Operating in the Minneapolis-St. Paul metropolitan area of approximately two million, it was one of the first such programs in a large urban jurisdiction. The center handled 903 case referrals during 1990 and 1991.

Oakland. The Victim Offender Reconciliation Program in Oakland serves the East Bay area of San Francisco. It was started in 1987 by the Office for Prisoner and Community Justice of Catholic Charities/Oakland Diocese. Both Alameda and Contra Costa counties are served by the program. Together, they are a large urban multicultural jurisdiction with a population of nearly two million. During 1990 and 1991, the program had 541 case referrals. Catholic Charities has worked on criminal justice matters for many years, offering a range of services and advocacy for prisoners, ex-offenders, and crime victims.

Austin. The Austin program, operated by the Travis County Juvenile Court in conjunction with the local Dispute Resolution Center, was added late in the study. Because the initial three sites are sponsored by private agencies, Austin offered an opportunity to compare the effects of public versus private victim-offender mediation programs on client satisfaction and perceptions of fairness. During 1990 and 1991, Austin had 1,107 case referrals.

FINDINGS

Data were collected from 1,153 interviews with crime victims and juvenile offenders in four states, reviews of program and court records, interviews with court officials and program staff, and observations of twenty-eight mediation sessions. The findings, while not necessarily generalizable to all victim-offender programs, help illustrate why restorative justice and mediation are receiving increased attention in many countries.

1. Mediation in juvenile proceedings results in very high levels of client satisfaction (victims, 79 percent; offenders, 87 percent) and perceptions of fairness (victims, 83 percent; offenders, 89 percent).

2. The process has a strong effect for both victims and juvenile offenders in humanizing the justice system response to crime.

3. Mediation reduces fear and anxiety among victims. Prior to mediation, nearly 25 percent of victims were afraid of being victimized again by the same offender. After mediation, only 10 percent were afraid of being revictimized.

4. Mediation has a significant impact on the likelihood that offenders will complete their restitution obligations (81

percent) to the victims, compared with similar offenders in court-administered programs without mediation (58 percent).

5. Juvenile offenders do not perceive mediation as a significantly less demanding response to their criminal behavior than other options available to the court. Mediation is consistent with efforts to hold young offenders accountable for their crimes.

6. Mediation has strong support from court officials, including both judges and probation staff, and is increasingly becoming institutionalized in juvenile courts.

7. Mediation is perceived to be voluntary by the vast majority (81 percent) of juvenile offenders who participated.

8. Mediation is perceived to be voluntary by the vast majority (93 percent) of victims who participated.

9. Victims in mediation were far more likely to experience the justice system as fair, compared with similar victims who went through the normal court process.

10. Considerably fewer and less serious additional crimes were committed within a one-year follow-up period by juvenile participants in mediation programs, compared with similar offenders who did not participate. Although consistent with two recent English studies, this important finding was not statistically significant because of the size of program samples.

IMPLICATIONS

The study provided strong empirical support to the emerging practice and theory of restorative justice. Mediation provides a radically different way to respond to certain types of crime. Crime victims and young offenders become active, rather than passive, participants in the justice process. Face-to-face mediation "breathes life" into the abstract notion that juvenile offenders need to be held accountable. Offenders are held accountable to the persons they victimized, not only to the state. Mediation also provides a mechanism for restoring emotional and material losses experienced by the victims, while offering offenders an opportunity to make amends in a very personal way.

Victim-offender mediation should be integrated more consistently into court-sponsored restitution programs. All restitution programs emphasize the importance of holding offenders accountable and compensating victims. Restitution is often ordered by juvenile courts but payment rates are often low. Offenders often perceive restitution, usually through payment to the court clerk, as a fine to pay the court rather than an obligation to the victim.

Mediation, by contrast, offers a process in which the offender is directly confronted with the realization of the victim as a "person" rather than simply an "object" or "target." The restitution obligation is negotiated with the victim. Likewise, after experiencing the offender as a "person" rather than simply as a "criminal," victims are often flexible in negotiating a plan for restitution that realistically reflects the offender's ability to pay.

Consideration should be given to substantial increases in the availability of victim-offender mediation services. Mediation can often be an appropriate intervention in a wide range of property offenses and assaults, including residential burglary and robbery, and with offenders with multiple prior convictions. Referral to mediation can be effective either as a diversion from prosecution or at a post-adjudication level.

Victim-offender mediation programs have limited scope in most jurisdictions, despite their growth in North America and Europe over the past decade and a growing body of research that indicates many positive benefits. Mediation should be made much more available to a wide range of victims and offenders in both property and violent crimes.

Restitution
Elmar Weitekamp

A restitution order requires the offender to reimburse the victim for the victim's losses. As a criminal sanction, restitution became popular in the 1970s and 1980s, often in association with mediation and victim-offender reconciliation. One review identified 940 recent publications on restitution.

In principle, the case for restitution is strong. It compensates the victim's loss; it is efficient; and it focuses the offender's attention on the wrongfulness of the crime and on its human consequences. It may provide a sense of vindication to the victim, of atonement to the offender, and of finality to both.

In practice, restitution programs have been plagued by problems. First, they are typically implemented and applied unsystematically. In Canada, for example, Bill C-89 provided the legal basis for widespread use of restitution as a penal sanction. However, Robinson's (1990) evaluation showed that use of restitution as a penal sanction did not increase substantially.

Second, most restitution programs are used only for property offenses, first-time offenders, or both. These limitations became common in the 1970s and 1980s and are now taken for granted.

Third, although advocates of restitution often intended that it be used as an alternative to incarceration, its use as an alternative is exceedingly rare. Instead, restitution, like community service, is commonly used as an add-on to probation and parole and expands rather than reduces control over the offender. Most evaluations show that community service is seldom used as an alternative to incarceration. Weitekamp (1990) found the same pattern to be true for restitution programs.

Fourth, restitution programs appear to favor white and middle-class offenders. Hudson and Galaway (1989) reported that restitution programs in Arizona, British Columbia, and Minnesota admitted disproportionately small numbers of minority offenders. Similar results have been obtained by many evaluators.

Fifth, a majority of restitution programs are designed for juveniles rather than adult offenders. Among juveniles in restitution programs, the majority are from white, middle-class backgrounds. Because juveniles and white middle-class offenders in general constitute low-risk groups, this suggests that officials do not envision restitution as a prison alternative.

Sixth, little evidence is available on the effects of restitution programs on recidivism rates, and such as exists is mixed. Hudson and Chesney (1978) reported that 6 percent of an experimental group in Minnesota (released from prison on probation to a restitution center) versus 24 percent of a control group (who served their prison sentences and were released on parole) were returned to prison following conviction for a new crime. However, only 10 percent of the control group were returned to prison for technical parole violations, compared to 40 percent of the experimental group, probably because the experimentals were under much tighter supervision, and this was responsible for their higher recidivism rate. Weitekamp (1990) found in Philadelphia that a restitution group, once they understood that their payments must be made, had a lower revocation rate compared to incarceration and probation-only groups.

Finally, a major problem of restitution programs is haphazard planning, implementation, and evaluation. Often, they have no concrete goals and are combined with other criminal-justice and welfare programs, making evaluations of their effects impossible. Furthermore, net-widening effects are seldom investigated. Major changes in planning and evaluation are essential.

Restitution in Philadelphia
Elmar Weitekamp

Restitution can be used as a sanction for serious offenders and for violent offenses. An evaluation of extensive use of restitution for serious offenders by Judge Lois Forer in the Philadelphia Court of Common Pleas shows that such offenders can satisfy restitution orders while achieving recidivism rates at least as good as those of comparable offenders who went to prison.

Intrigued by anecdotal reports on Judge Forer's use of restitution, I conducted a quantitative assessment of her sentencing from 1974 to 1984 to learn how often she used restitution sentences, for what kinds of cases, and with what results. Unlike formal programs in which risk screening typically limits participation to first-time offenders, property offenders, and predominantly white, middle-class offenders, Judge Forer's cases were assigned randomly to her and she imposed restitution sentences on her own initiative. Her caseload included mostly minority offenders. Half of the offenses were violent.

THE STUDY

Of the 567 sentenced offenders in my study, 198 were incarcerated, 173 received restitution, and 196 received probation. Three fifths had a prior arrest record, and nearly 30 percent had been incarcerated. Many charges were violent: homicide (5 percent), rape (4 percent), robbery (23 percent), and aggravated assault (20 percent). The rest consisted of burglaries, larcenies, and other less serious offenses. Weapon use and victim injury occurred in nearly half of the cases. Three quarters of the offenders were black and one fifth were white.

To determine which offenders received which sentences and why, I divided them into an incarceration group, a probation-with-restitution group, and a probation group, and collected information on their criminal histories, their current offenses, and their previous backgrounds. I employed a variety of statistical measures to analyze the data.

I collected revocation, reconviction, and reincarceration data for two years after sentencing for all offenders and found that more than 60 percent of those sentenced to restitution successfully completed their sentences. Initially, the restitution group had the highest percentage of revocation hearings

(51.0 percent), followed by probation (30.8 percent), and incarceration (27.8 percent). The results for the two latter groups are likely to be understated because a great deal of information was missing. Reasons for revocation hearings for the restitution group included commission of a new crime (35.4 percent) and technical violations (45.6 percent). However, in a third of those proceedings, a new probation term was imposed, and 61.7 percent of those offenders (roughly 10 percent of all restitution sentences) served their new terms successfully.

The offender profits from the imposition of a restitution sentence and the extended social control; because many revocation proceedings led to the imposition of new probation terms, offenders' obligations to make payments were emphasized.

THE RESULTS

The evaluation showed that Judge Forer ordered restitution as a sentence for quite serious crimes. Weapon use, whether an offense was a crime of violence or a property crime, gang membership, and victim injury made no consistent difference in whether Judge Forer imposed prison or restitution. Because these variables are usually used to determine the seriousness of a crime and the penal sanction, it was surprising that they made no difference and shows that restitution was ordered for serious crimes.

The only criminal history variables that were associated with whether Judge Forer ordered restitution were the presence (or absence) of prior arrests and whether the offender was jailed before trial. However, other important variables involving the existence and character of incarcerations, prior arrests, or convictions, had no consistent effect on the imposition of an incarceration sentence.

The only features of the current crime that were related to whether restitution was ordered were the small (under $500) or large (over $1,000) values of property offenses. Restitution was more likely in the former case and less in the latter. The extent of personal injuries had no consistent effect on the nature of the sentence, again showing use of restitution for serious crimes.

THE IMPLICATIONS

The results support wider use of restitution for more serious offenders than is now the case.

The increased use of restitution did not lead to heightened risks to public safety. Most offenders (61.2 percent) ordered to pay restitution completed their probation successfully, and only 24.5 percent were incarcerated. Compared to the general finding that 41 percent of released prisoners in the United States are reincarcerated within three years, society appears much better off using restitution as an alternative to incarceration.

2

COMMUNITY
SERVICE

Introduction

Community service is a much underused criminal sanction in the United States. Although one of the earliest organized community service programs was started in Alameda County, California, in 1966 for traffic offenders who would otherwise have gone to jail, the most extensive and systematic community service programs were established in England and Wales, and in Scotland. The English program, started on a pilot basis in 1973, was carefully evaluated by Home Office researchers and established nationwide soon thereafter. The defendant must have been convicted of "an offense punishable by imprisonment" (Pease 1985) and must perform 40 to 240 hours of work within one year. The evaluations, using a variety of research designs, concluded that recidivism rates for offenders sentenced to community service were neither better nor worse than those of comparable offenders receiving different sentences. They also concluded that the community sentence order, intended to be used in lieu of incarceration for many offenders, was applied nearly equally to offenders who would otherwise have been imprisoned and offenders who would otherwise have been sentenced to probation. (These findings—neither better nor worse recidivism rates and a 50/50 split in caseload between those drawn from prison and those

drawn from probation—recur throughout evaluations of intermediate sanctions over which judges have the principal power
of assignment.)

Researchers from the Vera Institute of Justice in New York
City established a pilot community service program in Bronx
County, New York, in 1979. On the basis of the most extensive
American evaluation of community service, they reached conclusions on net-widening and recidivism similar to the English
evaluation findings. The pilot program has been institutionalized in New York City. The program is intended for otherwise
jail-bound offenders and consists of seventy hours of supervised work on community or nonprofit-organization projects.
Failures to appear for work or to carry out assignments are
taken seriously and nonperformers are referred back to court;
revocation for nonparticipation generally results in a jail term.
By the late 1980s, the community service program was handling about 1,200 convicted offenders per year.

Both the English and New York City programs are intended
to be punitive and to serve as midlevel sanctions between
prison and probation. In New York City, probation caseloads
often run between 200 and 300 probationers per officer, and
the stereotype of "mere probation" appears too often to be
warranted. The Vera program was designed with repetitive
property offenders in mind—third-, fourth-, or fifth-time
felons for whom a sentence to probation no longer seems
appropriate but for whom a six-month jail term seems too
severe. The Vera program was designed to assure that such
offenders would receive a real sanction and that conditions
would be enforced. In England, probation caseloads are much
smaller than is common in the United States and the Probation
Service largely defines its role as social work and social support. Community service in New York, by contrast, was
intended to be burdensome and to have punitive bite, and
community service officers were expected not only to be
helpers but also to be enforcers.

Regrettably, organized community service has not caught

on in most American jurisdictions. Although judges often add a community service obligation to a probation sentence, few jurisdictions have created well-organized programs to assure that offenders are placed in work assignments, that work assignments are carried out, and that consequences attach to nonparticipation. Without an administrative apparatus and follow-up, community service sentences are no more credible than ordinary probation, and it should be no surprise that they are not widely seen as midlevel punishments.

That is a pity, because credible community service programs can play a number of different sanctioning roles. First, if financial sanctions come into wider use, community service can serve as a "fine on time" for indigents who cannot pay in cash. A 30-unit day fine translates easily into some number of days of community service. Second, for nondangerous repeat offenders, credible, enforced community service programs are a cost-effective alternative to short jail and prison sentences. Third, for some special types of offenders—for example, white-collar criminals or drug-abusing athletes—community service can provide symbolically powerful demonstrations of the consequences of those kinds of illegal behavior.

There are several reasons why community service has not caught on in this country. One is a failure to accept that any well-run program is expensive. In the early 1980s, for example, Vera's seventy-hour program cost $916 for each participating offender. That translates to nearly $20,000 per year per program slot, which seems a lot until it is compared to the $40,000 per year that New York City then spent for each jail bed. Nonetheless, as the cliche goes, you have to spend money to make money, and most jurisdictions are reluctant to invest the necessary funds to make community service effective.

Another impediment is the severity of jail and prison sentences in the United States. The 70-hour and 240-hour maximum community service orders in New York and England result from judgments about the practical limits of the capacity of public agencies to supervise and enforce compliance. If work orders are to be imposed by judges, they must be credible; to be credible, they must be enforced; thus acknowledgment of the practical limits of enforcement dictates the length of the work obligation. In the United States, however, six-, twelve-, and twenty-four-month sentences are commonly imposed on offenders who in other countries are sentenced to a few days or not at all. It is difficult to persuade a judge that a seventy-hour work obligation is an appropriate alternative to a six- or twelve-month jail term. This is especially true under sentencing guidelines systems.

A number of states have tried to incorporate community service into their guideline systems. Typically, as in Washington State, they have considered how to make community service equivalent to incarceration and have decided that one day's confinement equals one or even three days' community service. By the latter measure—that 24 hours' community service can substitute for one day in confinement—the New York program could be used in lieu of three days' jail and the English program in lieu of ten days'.

Nonetheless, our current knowledge about community service is important. The pressures of prison numbers and costs will lead to increased use of intermediate sanctions, as will a growing ambition by state sentencing guidelines commissions to incorporate intermediate sanctions into their guidelines schemes. When the time comes that policymakers are willing to invest adequate resources in community service, the work reported in the following articles by Douglas McDonald and Gill McIvor shows what must be done.

Community Service Sentences
Douglas C. McDonald

Community service orders—obligations to perform unpaid labor—are increasingly being used as a sentence by courts in this country and abroad.

Probably the first systematic use of the sanction was by the Alameda County (California) Court, which in 1966 devised a community service sentencing program to solve the problem posed by indigent women who violated traffic and parking laws. Too poor to pay a fine, these women were likely otherwise to be thrown in jail. By imposing community service orders, the courts were able to impose punishment while easing the suffering visited on the women's families, averting the cost to the public of imprisonment, and producing valuable services to the community at large. Alameda County's judges soon broadened the program to include male offenders, juveniles, and persons convicted of other, more serious crimes.

Community service sentences were given a big boost when the British government instituted a nationwide program in 1973. Within a few years, tens of thousands of offenders throughout the United Kingdom were placed on probation to work off community service obligations. This demonstrated the feasibility of using the sentence on a large scale, and similar programs sprang up in Australia, Canada, New Zealand, and the United States.

Since the end of the 1970s, the use of community service sentences, and the numbers of formally organized programs, have increased substantially. No surveys of adult programs have been done in the past decade, but there may be as many as 500. Judges in jurisdictions lacking formally organized programs often fashion community service sentences on their own. However, it is important to recognize that these programs have established little more than a beachhead in American courts. Only a small minority of the courts in this country order community service with any regularity, and the proportion of offenders receiving them is even smaller.

One barrier to broader acceptance of community service sentences has been the lack of agreement as to why the courts should impose them in the first place. Which objectives— punishment, rehabilitation, deterrence, incapacitation—

should judges try to achieve with them? Some argue that these sentences can serve several penal purposes simultaneously.

The missions of many programs are formulated in vague, abstract, and often idealistic terms. This results in considerable diversity of practice from one courthouse to another, and, not infrequently, confusion within jurisdictions regarding the proper and acceptable place of these sentences. To increase the odds of institutionalizing community service sentences, probably the surest course is to clarify why judges should impose them, under what conditions, and within what limits.

For more information on community service, see Norval Morris and Michael Tonry, *Between Prison and Probation: Intermediate Punishments in a Rational Sentencing System*, and Ken Pease, "Community Service Orders."

Community Service Sentencing in New York City
Douglas C. McDonald

In late 1978, New York City's Vera Institute of Justice began a small project in the Bronx Criminal Court to test the use of seventy hours of unpaid labor as a sentencing option. Within a few years, the project had spread to all the city's major misdemeanor courts. In 1989, community service orders (CSOs) became a fully institutionalized feature of the city's criminal-justice system, providing the courts the resources to impose 1,600 CSOs a year.

The project aimed to serve as a means of punishing chronic property offenders—mostly thieves—who otherwise would have been sentenced to short jail terms. It also provided a means of punishing offenders who would have gotten less onerous sentences for lack of suitable alternatives.

COMMUNITY SERVICE AS PUNISHMENT

Because New York City judges were imposing short jail terms principally for punishment, and because they had so few other unambiguously punitive options for misdemeanor offenses, Vera's planners decided that designing CSOs as alternative punishments would maximize the likelihood of adoption. To make it clear that CSOs were punitive in purpose and not designed to be rehabilitative, planners chose not to have CSOs imposed as a condition of probation. A legislative amendment was therefore sought, and won, that enabled the court to impose the sanction as a stand-alone punishment. Upon completion of the obligation (eight hours a day, five days a week, for two weeks straight), the offender fulfills the terms of the sentence.

The planners designed the sentence also as a way of stiffening the penalty imposed on offenders who would not otherwise have gone to jail. This was done partly because judges wanted such options. In addition, many in city government felt that too many criminal offenders were getting away with insufficient penalties because the courts and the correctional systems were overloaded and because judges had too few enforceable punishments at their disposal.

THE COURTS ADOPTED THE SENTENCE

The reception from district attorneys and administrative judges was enthusiastic. Judges complained that they had too few sentencing alternatives, and more were welcome. Prosecutors also recognized that serving time on the streets, where offenders were giving some value to the community, was an acceptable alternative to spending a few weeks or months in jail.

THE SERVICE OBLIGATION

Offenders perform mostly manual labor in crews supervised by project-employed foremen. The work is done for municipal government agencies or for not-for-profit organizations. Offenders help strip buildings being renovated by community development organizations in Harlem; they paint senior citizens' centers, install smoke alarms in community-owned nursing homes, paint and repair park benches, and clear debris from vacant city lots, among other types of labor. The work is onerous but not demeaning.

The CSO is strictly enforced. Offenders are permitted only a few unexcused absences. Any more absences result in the project's managers going to court to get a warrant issued for the rearrest and resentencing of the violator to jail. Because strict enforcement has been seen as the key to judicial acceptance, the project established its own warrant squad, composed of former law enforcement officers, all of whom are armed.

Completion rates have varied between 50 and 80 percent throughout most of the past ten years. Although seventy hours' labor may seem like a light punishment, many of those sentenced lead hard and often desperate lives, and find it difficult to complete the obligation while managing to keep themselves alive and fed. Surprising numbers of defendants have chosen instead to be sentenced to jail for upwards of six months because they thought they would not be able to perform the CSO sentence, and would then be sent to jail anyway.

EVALUATING THE EXPERIMENT

To see whether the program was having the desired effects, an extensive evaluation was undertaken. All the key players in three borough courts and projects were interviewed and observed in their work. Data were collected on cases given CSOs and those defendants screened but subsequently rejected. Once start-up uncertainties were past, evaluators found that—as intended—about half the offenders sentenced to CSOs thereby avoided jail terms and half would otherwise have received simple probation.

The evaluation also examined various costs and benefits of the CSO's use. Those given a CSO were rearrested at exactly the same rate as similar persons sent to jail for short terms and then released. Although some committed crimes that could have been prevented by jailing them instead, most crimes were the same sorts of relatively petty offenses that they had committed in the past. Unfortunately, because we lack capacity to predict which offenders will commit new crimes, the only way to avoid the risk of subsequent rearrest would be to jail all offenders convicted of misdemeanors. At the current annual cost of $50,000 per offender in New York City, such a policy would be impossible to implement. For crimes that are not grave but deserving of a response, an intermediate punishment such as community service may be justified.

Use of the sanction also provides other social utilities. Communities reap the fruit of unpaid labor. During 1984—a period assessed by the evaluators—offenders in the New York City project worked a total of 60,000 hours and provided perhaps a quarter of a million dollars' worth of services. In 1984, CSOs saved the city government approximately 102 prisoner-years of jail space.

Giving judges an additional sentencing option also permits them to better match the punishment to the crime. As the New York City experience shows, the creation of a sustainable and enforceable community service sentence can be accomplished.

For a fuller story of the Vera experiment and of its evaluation, see Douglas McDonald, *Punishment Without Walls: Community Service Sentences in New York City.* Information on the project's current operations is available from the Vera Institute, 377 Broadway, 11th Floor, New York, NY 10013; (212) 334-1300.

CSOs Succeed in Scotland

Gill McIvor

Community service in Scotland has proved to be a successful addition to the repertoire of sentences available to the Scottish courts. It has been applied with high completion rates across a wide range of offenders and offenses; is less costly than imprisonment; has clearly benefited the community and offenders themselves; and has, in some instances, had a longer-term impact upon offending behavior.

Community service by offenders was introduced in Scotland on an experimental basis in 1977, and schemes now exist throughout the country. The Scottish model closely resembles the approach developed in England and Wales in the early 1970s.

The Community Service by Offenders (Scotland) Act of 1978 permits offenders convicted of offenses punishable by imprisonment to be ordered instead to perform between 40 and 240 hours of unpaid work of benefit to the community. Unless an extension is granted by the court, the work must be completed within twelve months. Offenders who fail to comply with the requirements of their community service orders (for example, by regularly failing to turn up for work or by changing their address without notifying the community service scheme) can be returned to court and resentenced for the original offense.

Roughly half of offenders sentenced to community service in Scotland are sentenced in lieu of incarceration (recent legislation aims to increase that proportion). A comprehensive evaluation has shown that offenders sentenced to community service in Scotland have no worse recidivism rates than comparable imprisoned offenders, that some offenders (those who value the work) exhibit greatly reduced later property offending, and that offenders, social service agencies, judges, and service recipients tend by large proportions to find the program worthwhile and the services provided valuable.

TYPES OF PLACEMENTS

Most orders in Scotland are to one of two types of placement setting. In team placements (which nationally account for 64 percent of community service offenders), small groups of offenders—usually between four and six—carry out work for disadvantaged members of the public or for nonprofit community organizations that would be unable to perform the work themselves or to pay others to carry out certain essential tasks. Team placements are overseen by a skilled supervisor employed by the local community service scheme. Most involve practical tasks such as painting, decorating, gardening, and carpentry.

In agency placements, individual offenders provide services to nonprofit organizations such as residential homes for the elderly, youth clubs, or day-care facilities for children. Offenders are supervised by agency staff who are responsible for allocating tasks, monitoring work, and notifying the community service organizer if the offender misses an appointment, fails to obey instructions, or behaves in any way that gives cause for concern. By their nature, agency placements offer greater scope for offenders to do work that involves a more personalized component, though some employ offenders exclusively on practical tasks.

Scotland, unlike England and Wales, does not have a separate probation service to supervise offenders in the community. Social-work services to offenders and their families (including probation supervision and community service) are provided by social workers employed by local government agencies but funded in full by the central government.

SCALE AND FUNDING

The number of local schemes and the annual number of orders have grown steadily. From a modest base in 1981 of 1,226 orders, 5,045 community service orders were imposed in 1990, representing 2.7 percent of all individuals convicted in the criminal courts that year (Scottish Office 1992). The use of community service increased by 20 percent between 1989 and 1990 following the assumption by the central government of full funding responsibility. Central funding was accompanied by an increase in resources to meet the anticipated demand for community service orders. In the mid-to-late 1980s some

Part 2   Community Service

schemes (particularly those serving busy city courts) had been unable to keep up with demand for community service orders and for short periods had ceased making new referrals to keep workloads within manageable proportions.

EVALUATION RESEARCH

Despite the relatively modest scale of community service in Scotland (in comparison, say, to England and Wales, where in 1990 around 37,500 orders were made), community service in Scotland has been comprehensively evaluated over the last five years. The research program began with a comparison of the effectiveness of practice across twelve schemes and an examination of offenders' experiences and attitudes. There then followed a comparative cost analysis of community service and prison; a survey of placement agencies and individual members of the public who had been the recipients of unpaid work; a study of sentencers' views and use of community service; and, finally, an analysis of reconvictions among offenders who had participated in the earlier research.

Who gets community service in Scotland? Offenders who are sentenced to community service orders in Scotland are typically young, unemployed males. Most have at least one previous criminal conviction (with an average of around five), and just under a third have previously served a sentence of imprisonment or, in the case of those under twenty-one years of age, detention. They are most likely to have been sentenced for property offenses such as burglaries and thefts (56 percent of offenders), minor assaults (27 percent), road traffic offenses (13 percent), or breaches of public order (22 percent). Offenders are most likely to be rejected for community service because of substance abuse, poor response to previous community service or probation supervision, or failure to attend their assessment interviews.

Who is least likely to succeed? Around three quarters complete their community service orders successfully. One in seven is resentenced for failure to comply. The remainder have their orders terminated for such reasons as illness or imposition of a prison sentence that prevents completion of their hours within twelve months.

Offenders whose orders are revoked tend to have a higher number of previous convictions and more prior experience of custodial sentences. Revocation rates are higher among offenders who have unsettled addresses and who have no prior employment experience. Even so, most offenders who might be considered poorer bets complete their orders successfully: 71 percent who were assessed as having a high likelihood of failure completed their community service orders.

How do offenders view community service? Most regard community service as a relatively rewarding experience. Most in our study found their community service work to be interesting (88 percent) and enjoyable (91 percent). Many gained new skills, of either a practical or interpersonal nature, while completing their orders (69 percent), three quarters believed that they had gained something from being on community service, and most (88 percent) were willing to undertake community service again. Most offenders considered that community service had been worthwhile (88 percent) and that their work had benefited recipients (96 percent). Their experiences appear to have been especially rewarding if placements involved high levels of contact with the people who would benefit from their work, enabled them to acquire additional practical or interpersonal skills, or engaged them in tasks that they could readily recognize as being of value to recipients and, more important, were valued by recipients.

The survey of agencies offering placements revealed that in half of them at least one offender had continued to do volunteer work after completing the work ordered by the court. Nonetheless, few offenders considered community service to be an easy option. Three quarters experienced it as a punishment because of the discipline and commitment that completion of an order required, the intrusion into their leisure time, and the fact that the work was unpaid.

How do the courts view community service? Community service has proved to be a popular option among Scottish sentencers because it enables them to combine a punitive response with one that enables the community to benefit directly from unpaid work. Community service schemes were viewed by sentencers as offering an effective and credible option for the courts. In Scotland there is no requirement that offenders on community service provide work for the victims of their crimes, nor is any attempt made to match the type of work to the type of crime that the offender has been convicted of (for example, requiring that offenders who have been convicted of driving while intoxicated complete their hours in a hospital casualty department). Nonetheless, many sentencers believe that bringing offenders into contact with members of the community less advantaged than themselves may contribute to a changed outlook on the part of the offenders and may, in the longer term, lead to reductions in offending behavior.

How much does the community benefit? A majority of recipients appear to appreciate the work that is carried out by offenders. Individual recipients of work tend to be elderly, disabled, or suffering from ill health. Most found the work to be well supervised (96 percent), of a high standard (77 percent), and of considerable benefit to them (87 percent), and they were, with very few exceptions, willing to make use of their community service scheme again. The nonprofit agencies were likewise satisfied with their experiences of offering placements to community service offenders. Most believed that the offenders had helped to enhance the services they offered, and many thought that the offenders themselves had gained self-respect, confidence, or a sense of fulfillment from their work. Unexpected absences were, on occasion, a source of frustration for agencies, but most were prepared to continue offering placements to their local community service schemes.

Is it an alternative to prison? The original legislation did not contemplate the imposition of community service orders in lieu of other noncustodial penalties such as fines. Most sentencers, however, consider it inappropriate to restrict community service to offenders who would otherwise receive short prison sentences. Community service is used to an increased extent as an alternative to other noncustodial sanctions, and it was estimated that by 1986 slightly fewer than half the orders made (at most, perhaps 45 percent) had replaced sentences of imprisonment. Most offenders (89 percent), however, believed that they had been diverted from custody by their community service orders. In 1991 the enabling legislation was amended to require that the courts impose community service orders only upon offenders who are facing custodial sentences. It is still too early to establish the effects of that legislative change on sentencing practices.

Is it effective in reducing recidivism? Community service in Scotland is not premised on explicitly rehabilitative rationales but is widely believed, if imaginatively organized, to be rehabilitative in effect. The frequency of reconviction was lower among offenders who had found their community service experience to be particularly worthwhile: those who were reconvicted averaged 2.9 new convictions in the following three years, compared with an average of 4.6 reconvictions among offenders whose experiences were less rewarding. The most dramatic impact was upon property offenses. Even though they were as likely to have been convicted of property offenses in the past or to have been sentenced to community service orders for property offenses, only 39 percent of offenders who had valued their experience of community service were reconvicted of property offenses, compared with 70 percent of offenders whose experiences of community service were less worthwhile. This suggests that some offenders may have come to appreciate the impact of their offending upon others even more disadvantaged than themselves.

Is it more cost-effective than prison? When both direct and indirect costs are taken into account, an average-sized community service order (of approximately 140 hours) was less costly than a likely alternative prison sentence (of around four and three-quarter months): the former was estimated to cost £1,044 (approximately $1,670) and the latter £2,268 ($3,630) at 1987 prices. There was no evidence, moreover, that community service was any less effective than imprisonment in reducing subsequent recidivism: the 63 percent reconviction rate after three years following community service compares favorably with rates of reconviction following imprisonment or following other sentences designed to divert offenders from custodial sentences.

The popularity of community service with the judiciary has been a two-edged sword since it has, on occasion, resulted in the imposition of relatively demanding sentences for comparatively trivial offenses. Time alone will tell whether the greater consistency of sentencing practice that is hoped for will be achieved by the legislative changes that have recently been introduced.

3

INTENSIVE
SUPERVISION
AND
ELECTRONIC
MONITORING

Introduction

Intensive supervision probation and parole, commonly called ISP, was the most ubiquitous of the intermediate sanctions of the 1980s. There were three broad types, all characterized by smaller-than-normal caseloads, typically two officers to twenty-five offenders. Most involved numerous conditions including frequent unannounced drug testing, community service, house arrest, and two to five face-to-face contacts per week with the probation officers.

The best known programs were "front-end" prison diversion programs in which judges sentenced prison-bound offenders to ISP. Georgia's program was much the best known and most replicated. This was largely the result of extensive publicity and an in-house evaluation, which concluded that most probationers in the program had indeed been diverted from prison and that, compared with offenders who were sent to prison, the ISP offenders had a low failure rate (16 percent) and very few arrests for serious crimes. At one time, Georgia corrections officials claimed that ISP obviated the need to build two new prisons.

With the passage of time, the Georgia program's apparent remarkable success has become less believable. Contrary to the initial reports, it is now widely believed that the program's low recidivism and failure rates resulted from the low-risk nature of the offenders sentenced to ISP. Although program policies directed judges to sentence only prison-bound offenders to ISP, nothing prevented judges from sentencing to the program offenders who otherwise would have received probation, and this appears to be what happened. In part because of the Georgia example, we now understand that prison-diversion programs should have high failure and rearrest rates. If prison-bound offenders tend to be relatively high risks for recidivism, a program that genuinely diverts offenders from prison can be expected to have high recidivism rates. The converse also is true. A purported prison-diversion program with low failure and recidivism rates is probably not diverting many offenders from prison.

"Back-end" ISP programs, in which prisoners were released early directly into ISP, were less common but followed a similar trajectory. The best-known program, in New Jersey, was even more intensive than Georgia's ISP. Offenders were subject to thirty-one probation-officer contacts a month (including twelve face-to-face, seven for curfew checks, and four for urinalysis), and were selected from among prisoners who applied for acceptance into the program and survived a seven-step screening process. The initial evaluations concluded that the program was achieving lower recidivism rates than experienced by comparable inmates after release and that the program was saving New Jersey money.

As was true with Georgia, after a time most of the claims for the program's success became less convincing. The comparison groups that had exhibited higher recidivism rates proved not so comparable after all; they were on average higher-risk offenders (this also happened in Georgia). The screening process for admission was so stringent that it soon appeared that the program was in effect releasing low-risk offenders from prison who probably should not have been sent there in the first place. Because ISP conditions were vigorously enforced, the program had nearly a 50 percent failure and revocation rate, mostly for technical violations, which seriously undermined the goal of a substantial net savings in prison beds. Finally, although at first glance a prison release program looks by definition to achieve 100 percent diversion from prison, it was soon appreciated that the issue was more complicated. The prison-bed savings claim is based on the assumption that the creation of the program would not cause judges to send low-risk offenders to prison for a "short sharp shock" in the belief that they would promptly be released to ISP. This is disingenuous, and Rutgers University's Todd Clear soon showed that a tiny percentage increase in incarceration of low-risk offenders would swamp any prison-bed savings attributable to ISP.

The third form of ISP, used both in probation and parole agencies, was a form of case management in which officials using prediction instruments assigned higher-risk inmates to closer supervision. This is the least innovative form of ISP and seems little more than the combination of rational bureaucratic management with the growing technology of empirically based statistical risk predictions. Similar programs were tested in the 1950s and 1960s, when probationers were assigned to caseloads of different sizes in the hope that more intensive supervision would result in lower recidivism rates. The rationales were different. The earlier programs had rehabilitative goals; the hypothesis was that offenders in smaller caseloads would receive more assistance and should accordingly be more likely to reestablish law-abiding habits. The more recent programs had crime control goals; the hypothesis was that closer scrutiny would have some deterrent effects and would more quickly discover violation conditions and new crimes, thereby more promptly getting unsuccessful probationers off the streets. Evaluations of both kinds of case management ISP concluded that they had no effects on recidivism rates.

After more than a decade of evaluation research of steadily increasing rigor and sophistication, we now know a great deal about ISP of all three types. The RAND Corporation conducted an experimental evaluation of fourteen ISP programs of all types in nine states. Offenders who satisfied eligibility criteria were randomly assigned to the ISP program or to whatever sanction they would otherwise have received. The findings are not unlike those reported in the introduction to the community service chapter. Participation in the ISP programs had no significant effect on recidivism rates in relation to new crimes (though closer supervision did result in higher rates of technical violations and revocations). Particularly telling for front-end programs that depend on judges to divert prison-bound offenders, the RAND evaluations of the only two front-end prison diversion programs broke down because judges refused to honor the random allocation system and often insisted on imprisoning offenders who met program eligibility guidelines and were randomly assigned to ISP.

Richard Will's articles in this section give a fuller introduction to ISP programs, and the article on evaluations by Joan Petersilia and Susan Turner summarizes the findings from the RAND evaluation. The articles on electronic monitoring document the seemingly inexorable spread of that technology throughout the American corrections system and steady advances in technological sophistication. In England and Wales, interestingly enough—as the article by George Mair reports— the Home Office conducted an evaluation of a modest pilot project, and, in its aftermath, decided not to adopt electronic monitoring.

Intensive Supervision

Intensive Supervision Probation
Richard Will

Intensive supervision probation, commonly called ISP or IPS, combines traditional probation services with close surveillance. Many programs have probationer:staff ratios of 10:1 or 25:2.

Experiments with use of low ratios of offenders to officers is not new. During the 1950s and 1960s there was substantial experimentation with differential caseloads. Evaluations generally found that low caseloads did not produce lowered recidivism rates.

Today, ISP's most often declared purpose is to provide a credible community sanction at less cost than incarceration and without endangering public safety. Probation's traditional emphasis on rehabilitation has been replaced with a concern for punishment and incapacitation. ISP programs typically include unscheduled drug-use checks, electronic monitoring, counseling, fees-for-services, mandatory employment, community service, unannounced home visits, curfews, and strict revocation procedures.

Implemented in at least forty states, ISP is one of the most widely adopted intermediate sanctions of the 1980s. Its "get tough" philosophy holds great appeal to many. Its use as a mechanism to relieve prison crowding appeals to a much wider audience.

ISP programs take three broad forms. In New Jersey, for example, ISP is a mechanism for early release from prison. In Georgia and Illinois, ISP is intended to provide a credible alternative to incarceration for otherwise prison-bound offenders. In Massachusetts, ISP is a case management tool used to

achieve closer controls and surveillance for higher-risk probationers.

In practice, there is no generic form of ISP. The amount of
prescribed supervision varies considerably by jurisdiction.
Daily face-to-face contacts between the offender and his or
her ISP probation officer may be required for high-risk clients
in Georgia. Thirty-one contacts per month, with twelve of
them being face-to-face, are required in New Jersey. And in
Massachusetts, supervision included ten contacts per month
(four direct and six collateral). Some ISP programs, however,
require only two or three contacts per month. Program details
vary substantially among jurisdictions. Some focus primarily
on control and surveillance. Others offer extensive helping
services. Some use two-officer teams, one member specializing
in surveillance and control, the other in helping services.

The evaluation literature on ISP is perhaps the most extensive for any of the community sanctions in use today. The
most often studied and reported measures of ISP success
include whether offenders were appropriately selected,
whether programs are cost-effective, and whether recidivism
has been reduced. The criteria selected to evaluate these
measures are often program-specific, so that making comparisons with other programs is not easy.

It is frequently difficult to determine whether ISP clients
are, indeed, chosen from the appropriate offender population.
Some of the questions that have been asked are: Were most of
the offenders truly prison bound? Were candidates chosen
from a population of high-risk offenders? Answers to these
questions from ISP evaluations conducted in California and
Massachusetts have been affirmative. In Georgia and other
states the results are more equivocal. The relevant policy
question is whether ISP contributes to widening the net of
social control rather than to conserving scarce prison space.

The results of cost-benefit analyses of ISP are ambiguous.
Appropriate analyses need to consider a complex set of interre-
lated variables that are extremely difficult to identify and

measure. In addition to the direct costs of stepped-up supervision and administration, the cost calculus is incomplete without consideration of indirect measures such as fees paid for service, the value of labor for community service, the value of family support provided while the offender remains in the community, the costs of revocation and resentencing, and the costs of new crime committed while serving an ISP sentence.

Recidivism studies offer mixed results. Some studies report that ISP offenders pose no more of a threat to the community than do regular probationers. This may be because the two populations are selected from the same pool of low-risk candidates or because close surveillance prevents new offenses by higher-risk offenders. Other studies show that ISP offenders exhibit higher rates of recidivism than do regular probationers. This may mean that such programs are handling higher-risk offenders and diverting offenders from prison.

Despite considerable variation in ISP purpose and practice, and the difficulties that surround evaluations of its success, it is clear that ISP is here to stay. It has wide acceptance in the courts and probation departments. In addition, evaluations have not disproven the claims of ISP proponents, although they have shown the need for more rigor in evaluation research—some examples of which are now entering the literature.

California ISP Programs Evaluated
Richard Will

In a landmark evaluation of three California ISP programs, RAND Corporation researchers Joan Petersilia and Susan Turner present mixed findings on ISP's effectiveness. ISP by itself did not appear to reduce recidivism rates but did appear capable of achieving cost savings. Close supervision combined with treatment and counseling may reduce recidivism rates. Funding was provided by the Bureau of Justice Assistance

(BJA) as part of an initiative in 1986 to support fourteen ISP demonstration projects in nine states. The RAND researchers evaluated programs in Contra Costa, Ventura, and Los Angeles Counties, California; all used ISP as a probation enhancement rather than as a diversion from prison.

EVALUATION PLAN

What makes the RAND evaluation significant is that, unlike most other ISP evaluations, it employed a randomized experimental design. Once eligibility for the ISP programs in Los Angeles and Contra Costa Counties was determined, offenders were randomly assigned to ISP (the experimental group) or routine probation (the control group). In Ventura, the control group consisted of the existing ISP program, in which supervision and program requirements were less demanding than those for the demonstration project.

The ISP programs were tailored to the local conditions regarding needs and risks assessments of offenders, financial resources, and political contexts. The three ISP programs all featured reduced caseloads compared with regular probation, three phases of supervision with graduated decreases in weekly face-to-face and telephone contacts, drug testing and counseling, and job referrals. The Los Angeles program also included an experimental group subject to electronic monitoring.

The evaluation covered the period between January 1987 and July 1988 and included a one-year follow-up of each participant beginning on the day of assignment to either the experimental or control group. Sample sizes varied between 152 and 170 individuals among the three sites. In general, about 75 percent of the participants scored "high" or "intensive" on an objective risk assessment, more than half had previously been in jail or prison, and nearly half had a serious drug problem.

EVALUATION FINDINGS

The RAND evaluation had several objectives. The first was to determine whether the ISP programs functioned as designed.

Although ISP clients had more contacts with officers than did their probation counterparts, the numbers were fewer than originally planned. Participation in treatment and counseling programs was lower than planned, but this often resulted from a lack of available treatment slots or from long waiting lists.

Second, recidivism rates were examined after one year for the ISP and control samples. No significant differences were found in the number of new arrests or the severity of offenses for new arrests between the groups at any of the sites.

The findings on recidivism rates result, the researchers argue, from the exceedingly high-risk population of offenders eligible for ISP programs in California—even more at risk for future crimes than offenders in prison diversion ISP programs in other states.

One important conclusion is that increased supervision alone had little effect on offenders' criminality. However, statistical analyses did reveal a relationship between participation in treatment and counseling and recidivism: all things being equal, greater participation was associated with lower recidivism rates.

Third, the average cost per offender on ISP was $7,240–$8,902 per year, compared to $4,923–$7,123 per offender per year in regular probation. ISP costs, however, are substantially lower than annual costs per offender in California jails and prisons. The higher ISP costs were attributed to expenses associated with closer supervision and to court costs for reprocessing recidivists.

CONCLUSIONS

At first glance, the California findings are not very supportive of the use of ISP with high-risk offenders. However, some of the results offer positive insights for the future. First, even though high violation rates are to be expected for high-risk clients placed on ISP, the diversion of low-risk, prison-bound offenders to community-based programs may achieve substantial cost savings. Second, although supervision alone does not appear to affect recidivism, supervision combined with treatment and counseling may reduce recidivism rates. Third, and perhaps most important, the evaluation findings strongly suggest that some funds now expended on monitoring and incarcerating high-risk offenders for technical violations might be spent more productively on drug and alcohol treatment and job placement.

Copies of the report, numbered R-3936-NIJ/BJA, are available for $18.00 from RAND's publication department, 1700 Main St., P.O. Box 2138, Santa Monica, CA 90407-2138.

Evaluating Intensive Supervision Probation and Parole
Joan Petersilia and Susan Turner

A recently completed RAND evaluation of intensive supervision parole and probation (ISP) programs shows that ISP is successful at some things—notably achieving closer surveillance and control of offenders—and there is some indication that ISP makes offenders likelier to participate in treatment and that treatment participation is associated with lower recidivism. The evaluation also shows, however, that ISP by itself seldom achieves other things—reduced recidivism, reduced prison populations, lower costs—that it is widely believed to achieve.

The RAND evaluation was an experiment in which offenders in fourteen ISP programs in nine states were randomly assigned to ISP or to whatever the conventional disposition would otherwise have been. The programs were funded by the Bureau of Justice Assistance (BJA) as part of a nationwide demonstration project.

THE RATIONALE FOR ISP

There are two main arguments for ISP. One is practical: prisons are overcrowded and resources are constrained. Some advocates claim that ISP can alleviate prison crowding at less than the cost of expanding prison capacity without jeopardizing public safety. The second is principle: ISP provides more latitude for making the punishment fit the crime, thus achieving punishments that are appropriately scaled to the offender's desert.

The practical argument has been most often used. ISP's ubiquity and popularity are based on a widespread belief that ISP programs alleviate prison crowding, cost less than incarceration, and control crime. However, the RAND results refute that belief:

> The programs did not alleviate prison crowding and may have increased it in some states.
>
> They cost considerably more than is generally realized.
>
> They were no more effective than routine probation and parole in reducing recidivism.

What the programs we studied did achieve was control—in each site, ISP was more punitive than routine probation and parole. To many, the terms *probation* and *parole* suggest support and services to offenders. Modern ISP programs do not always provide additional support, treatment, and services to offenders. The BJA programs were oriented more toward "surveillance and supervision" than "service and treatment." Stepped-up surveillance and frequent drug tests led to increased violation and incarceration rates, which drove up ISP program and court costs.

The evaluation findings show that the more stringently ISP programs enforce their punitive conditions, the more likely they are to exacerbate prison crowding and to approach the costs of imprisonment. Jurisdictions need seriously to consider what they want ISP to accomplish before investing further in it.

THE ISP DEMONSTRATION

In 1986, BJA solicited proposals from jurisdictions interested in participating in an experimental evaluation of ISP. BJA stipulated only that the sites focus on adults, exclude offenders convicted of violent crimes, and participate in an independent experimental evaluation. All other policy and operational decisions were left to the participating agencies.

The aim was to determine how participation in ISP programs affected the subsequent behavior of offenders. The experiment ran from 1986 through 1990 and involved nearly 2,000 offenders.

The sites tested ISP programs of three kinds: prison diversion, enhanced probation, and enhanced parole. Prison diversion ISP substitutes a community-based option for a prison term. Enhanced probation and parole programs increase surveillance and services for serious offenders already on probation and parole. The fourteen programs were representative of ISP across the country, including not only different types of ISP but different levels of offender risk, different contexts (political, financial, etc.), and different levels of government.

Only two sites—Marion County, Oregon, and Milwaukee, Wisconsin—implemented prison diversion programs. The rest were enhancement programs. Some used electronic monitoring (e.g., Macon, Georgia, and Des Moines, Iowa). Some used on-site drug testing (e.g., Atlanta). Others mandated treatment participation (e.g., Santa Fe). Some had a lengthy intensive phase, with successful offenders then being transferred to routine supervision (e.g., Los Angeles). Still others placed existing supervision "failures" in the most intensive phase (e.g., Houston).

Participating offenders varied. At some sites, offenders with any sex-offense history were excluded (e.g., Milwaukee); others accepted them (e.g., Ventura). All programs excluded offenders convicted of violent crimes, but many permitted offenders with prior violent convictions (e.g., Los Angeles). The sample included mostly felons convicted of burglary, theft, and drug offenses; a small but significant proportion had been convicted of more serious crimes.

Many correctional evaluations fail because the programs

evaluated are implemented poorly or not at all. Most of the ISP programs were implemented rather well. The one area in which most fell short concerned treatment. For a variety of reasons, many participating offenders were not provided drug, alcohol, and other treatment. This was true even when treatment was a condition of participation in ISP.

The sites followed identical procedures regarding random assignment and data collection. Once staff determined that an offender met local eligibility criteria, RAND staff assigned them randomly to ISP or otherwise. This was crucial because most previous ISP evaluations did not use random assignment, and positive outcomes could as easily result from less serious offenders being assigned as from the program itself. Random assignment helps ensure that the outcomes of different programs (e.g., recidivism rates) result from the programs and not from systematic biasing factors (e.g., less serious offenders being assigned to ISP).

Each offender was tracked for one year. Detailed data were collected on individual backgrounds, services received, and one-year outcome measures (including recidivism and social adjustment indicators).

COMMITMENTS TO PRISON

We cannot say whether prison diversion ISP might reduce prison crowding. The two sites that attempted such programs had problems that made the results equivocal. However, those problems—and that only two sites were willing to try prison diversion—suggest that ISP's potential as a prison diversion is probably limited.

Prison Diversion ISP. Experience in Milwaukee and Marion County shows how difficult it would be to reduce prison crowding through ISP. Eligibility requirements were so stiff in Marion County that few offenders qualified. In Milwaukee, judges and probation/parole officers often overrode the random assignments.

In Marion County, the original pool of eligible offenders

consisted of all adults facing sentence for nonviolent offenses whose presentence investigation recommended prison. During the ten-month period, 160 candidates met the criteria. After screening by Marion County community corrections staff, ISP staff, and the district attorney, only 36 candidates remained. However, the local judge was willing to divert offenders from prison to ISP only if they agreed. A quarter of the offenders refused. The resulting sample was too small to yield statistically meaningful results.

The Milwaukee experiment included two groups of offenders: front-end cases (i.e., high-risk offenders newly convicted of nonviolent felonies) and back-end cases (i.e., probation or parole violators facing revocation for new nonviolent felonies or technical violations). RAND randomly assigned approximately half of each group to ISP and half to prison. However, the ultimate sentencing was controlled by judges for the front-end cases and by the probation/parole officer for back-end cases.

Regardless of the random assignment, most front-end cases were sentenced to prison. Judges were unwilling to divert half of these serious offenders to a community alternative. The back-end experimental cases were placed on ISP as recommended, but fewer than half of the others were sent to prison. The rest were placed on routine probation or parole. These overrides foiled the experiment. We could no longer assume that the outcomes reflected program effects rather than the selection process.

Prison Crowding. Probation/parole enhancement ISP can exacerbate prison crowding. In general, ISP programs produced more technical violations and placed more offenders in prison or jail for those violations than did routine supervision.

Results in Texas are illustrative. Houston established a parole-enhancement program intended to reduce recommitments to the state prisons. The target group was parolees with the highest probability of returning to prison if left on current caseloads. Of the ISP offenders in Houston, 80 percent had technical violations, compared with one third of those on routine parole; nearly twice as many ISP offenders were returned to prison. Despite the program's intent, putting people on ISP added more offenders to the prison population than routine parole did.

COSTS

ISP is more expensive than is generally known. ISP, particularly enhancement programs, does not appear to have immediate cost-saving potential.

Our cost analysis estimated the total criminal-justice dollars spent on each offender during the one-year follow-up period, including the costs of correctional supervision and the court costs associated with reprocessing recidivists. In no instance did ISP programs result in cost savings, even when, as in Texas, they were designed to do so. At most sites, ISP resulted in more technical violations, more court appearances, and more incarcerations than did the conventional program—resulting in costs up to twice as high as for routine supervision. The principal variation in program costs is related to what the ISP program does about violations. If violations were ignored, program costs were lower; if not, costs were higher.

Imprisonment vs. ISP. In Oregon, ISP costs per offender are about 75 percent of the cost of sending an offender to prison—not a great savings. These costs reflect a crossover effect. That is, for the study period, ISP offenders and those sent originally to prison (the controls) spent about equal amounts of time incarcerated and on the street. Although the average nominal prison sentence for the Oregon group was five years, almost half were released after less than six months.

Routine Probation vs. ISP. For California's three enhancement programs, high violation and incarceration rates for ISP offenders drove up the estimated costs, which averaged $7,240 to $8,902 per offender for the year, compared with $4,923 to $7,123 in the control groups.

Routine Parole vs. ISP. In Houston, the estimated costs per offender were $6,778 for ISP, compared with $3,960 for the control group. This reflects higher rates of technical violations and recommitments to prison for the ISP offenders.

REDUCING RECIDIVISM

ISP participants were not arrested less often or have a longer time to failure than the control groups; nor were they arrested for less serious offenses. In eleven of the fourteen sites, arrest rates were somewhat higher for the ISP participants than for the control group. At the end of one year, 37 percent of the ISP participants and 33 percent of the control offenders had been arrested. If technical violations are taken as a recidivism measure, the record for ISP looks grimmer: an average of 65 percent of ISP clients had a technical violation, compared with 38 percent of the controls.

These findings should be interpreted with caution. Recorded recidivism may not be as accurate an indicator of an individual's criminality as it is of the ISP program's effects on the criminal-justice system. Officially recorded recidivism measures enforcement—the system's ability to detect crime and act on it (through arrests and technical violations).

Surveillance may be so stringent in an ISP program as to increase the probability that crimes (and technical violations) will be detected and an arrest made. It is possible that ISP offenders commit no more or fewer crimes than do offenders on routine supervision, but have a higher probability of being arrested for them.

TREATMENT

Treatment and service components in the ISP programs included drug and alcohol counseling, employment, community service, and payment of restitution. On many of these measures, ISP offenders participated more than did control group members; participation in such programs was correlated with reduced recidivism in some sites.

Aggregated data from all sites revealed that participation in counseling was not high in the experimental or control groups, but it was higher for ISP offenders. Forty-five percent of ISP offenders received some counseling during the follow-up period, compared with 22 percent of the controls.

Overall figures indicate that more than half of the ISP participants were employed, compared with 43 percent of the offenders on routine supervision.

Both the ISP offenders and the controls had low rates of restitution and even lower rates for community service. With the exception of the three Georgia sites, the rates of community service ranged from 0 to 16 percent for ISP and from 0 to 12 percent for the control programs. For both groups, the Georgia sites had rates in the 60-to-90-percent range. Restitution rates were uneven across the sites: for both groups, the percentage making restitution ranged from 0 to 42 percent.

Analyses of programs in California and Texas showed a relationship between treatment participation and recidivism. Higher levels of program participation were associated with a 10-to-20-percent reduction in recidivism. However, this analysis is not based on random assignments to treatment, and we do not know whether the lower recidivism was the effect of the treatment or of selection bias.

The evaluated programs were oriented more toward surveillance than treatment, with funds used largely for staff salaries rather than for treatment services. Sites had to rely on existing treatment programs, which in some cases were minimal. This raises the question of whether treatment participation would have been higher (and recidivism lower) had more treatment been available.

ISP AS "INTERMEDIATE PUNISHMENT"

If intensity is equated with punishment, the evaluated ISP programs qualify as intermediate punishments. They were much more stringent than routine probation and delivered more contacts and monitoring and more drug and alcohol testing.

Some people do not consider ISP a punishment, believing that offenders who remain in the community are not being punished. That may reflect the law-abiding citizen's perspective but not necessarily the criminal's. Interviews with offenders suggest that many offenders view ISP as more punitive than prison.

Norval Morris and Michael Tonry (1990) state that

> Convicted criminals should not be spared punitive responses to their crimes; there is no point in imposing needless suffering, but effective sentencing will normally involve the curtailment of freedom either behind walls or in the community, large measures of coercion, and enforced diminutions of freedom; this is entirely properly regarded as punishment. (p. 5)

Compared with the control programs, the ISP programs met that conception of punishment. Most had significantly higher levels of features that curtail freedom: face-to-face contacts, telephone and collateral contacts, law-enforcement checks, employment monitoring, and drug and alcohol testing. In thirteen sites, technical violations were higher for ISP than for the controls. In twelve sites, revocations to jail or prison were higher for ISP.

Legislators, justice system officials, and the public frequently ask, "Does ISP work?" and "Should we continue investing in it?" The ISP demonstration cannot answer such questions. Whether ISP can be said to "work" and whether states should begin or continue to invest in ISP depends on the answers to state policy questions—for example:

What is ISP expected to accomplish?
To which goals should highest priority be given?
Would the public support those priorities?
How should outcomes be judged?
Are the costs affordable?

If a jurisdiction is primarily interested in providing a continuum of punishments so that sentences can be tailored more closely to fit offenders' crimes, then ISP holds promise. If the primary goals are to reduce recidivism and costs, then ISP programs, as currently structured, will likely fall short.

These observations apply to other intermediate and alternative sanctions. Interest in boot camps, electronic monitoring, house arrest programs, and day-reporting centers is growing as jurisdictions search for innovative ways to punish offenders in the community. Proponents argue that such alternatives will relieve prison crowding, enhance public safety, and rehabilitate offenders—and all at a cost savings.

Intermediate sanctions probably cannot accomplish such ambitious goals. If community sanctions are made more effective by emphasizing public safety and offender accountability, an increase in program costs—not a decrease—is likely to occur. However, development of an array of sentencing options is an important and necessary first step toward creating more comprehensive and graduated sentencing systems. This goal—of helping to restore the principle of just deserts to the criminal justice system—provides the justification for continued development of ISP and other intermediate sanctions.

Electronic Monitoring

Electronically Monitored Home Detention
Terry L. Baumer and Michael G. Maxfield

For all practical purposes, electronic monitoring equipment first became commercially available around the beginning of 1985. Fueled by pressure of overcrowded institutions, limited budgets, and beliefs about the infallibility of computerized technology, electronically monitored home detention was quickly embraced by a wide variety of agencies. A survey conducted by Marc Renzema in February 1990 identified programs in each of the fifty United States. This survey also found that home detention was being applied to individuals at every stage of the criminal-justice process. Although early programs tended to target convicted individuals who would otherwise be sent to prison, recent initiatives have focused on clients who are released directly from prison or jail.

To understand electronically monitored home detention, it is important to distinguish between the sanction (home detention) and the method of monitoring compliance (electronic monitoring).

Home detention involves a legally imposed order for the individual to remain at home during specified hours of the day. The sanction usually allows for approved absences for employment, education, court-ordered treatment programs, and religious services. Other exceptions, such as errand time and passes, are less common. Additional controls, such as restrictions on visitors and alcohol prohibition, vary by program. Home detention is used both as a primary sanction and as an element of other intermediate alternatives, such as ISP.

There are several ways to monitor compliance with the home detention order. At its simplest, compliance can be monitored manually through a combination of field visits and telephone calls. Such methods are labor intensive and personnel dependent. Electronic monitoring equipment is designed to automate much of the monitoring process.

Two basic types of electronic monitoring systems, programmed contact and radio frequency, are now in use; there are many vendors and several proprietary variations on the basic approach.

PROGRAMMED CONTACT SYSTEMS

Programmed contact systems monitor compliance through telephone contacts randomly generated by a host computer. Program personnel maintain the computer equipment, enter client schedules, determine the intensity of contacts, and review information generated by the system. The computer uses telephone lines and attempts periodically to contact the client. When the telephone is answered, the client is directed to perform certain tasks designed to verify his or her presence. At this point there are several variations including voice stress analysis and video images, but the most common method includes an electronic "key" strapped to the offender. At the conclusion of the sequence, the computer program compares the actual response to the expected response and produces a status report. In theory, program personnel are immediately notified if the client is not home at the appointed time. The rationale for these systems is that the unpredictability of the contact schedule, combined with the threat of sanctions, will deter clients from unauthorized absences.

RADIO FREQUENCY SYSTEMS

Radio frequency systems require that a transmitter with a limited range be strapped to the individual being monitored. A receiver/dialer is connected to the telephone and monitors the presence of the individual through the signals emitted by the transmitter. This remote unit periodically uses telephone lines to contact the host computer. Program personnel must maintain the computer equipment, enter client schedules, and review information produced by the computer. When contacted by a remote unit, the host computer compares the information received with the stored schedule and produces a status report. The basic purpose of radio frequency systems is to provide information, approaching real-time reports, about offender compliance with detention conditions.

HYBRID SYSTEMS

Hybrid electronic monitoring systems are also now available. These operate primarily as a radio frequency system. When the remote unit reports an irregularity, such as an unauthorized absence, the host computer switches to a programmed contact mode and attempts to contact the client. If the programmed contact mode confirms the exit report, the system produces a violation notice for program personnel.

COST SAVINGS AND PRISON CROWDING

Electronic monitoring programs can provide some relief from institutional crowding. There is, however, very little evidence that this goal has been achieved. Programs into which offenders are released from jail or prison offer the most promise in this area, but most programs are small and can provide only limited relief. It is important to note that if violations are sanctioned with terms of incarceration, it is theoretically possible for a program to aggravate institutional crowding.

When calculated on a cost-per-client basis, electronic monitoring programs almost always appear to be a cost-effective alternative to incarceration. However, this outcome is an artifact of the way in which the costs are calculated. Unless the new electronic monitoring program will completely recover its cost through user fees, prevent construction of a new facility, or allow the jurisdiction to close an existing facility, there will almost always be a net additional cost to the jurisdiction. In estimating cost effectiveness it is advisable to look at the total correctional budget with and without (also before and after) the proposed program.

Introduction

PROGRAM PLANNING

Electronically monitored home detention programs require extensive organizational effort. Effective implementation involves considerably more than turning a computer on, pushing a few buttons, and going home. The electronic monitoring equipment requires a unique configuration of tasks and requisite skills. Many agencies with limited computer experience are not prepared and do not anticipate either the nature of the tasks or the labor required to deliver a credible program. For this reason some agencies subcontract the electronic monitoring service to a private monitoring company.

Electronic monitoring programs are not secure alternatives to incarceration. All programs attempt to deter unauthorized absences through the threat of detection and subsequent sanctions. However, there are no physical restraints. In this sense, the incapacitation provided by electronic monitoring programs is entirely voluntary. In effect, this means that the appropriate target population for these programs should be individuals who are not thought to pose a serious threat to others. Of course, this also means that some offenders will violate conditions, abscond, and commit new offenses.

In designing an electronic monitoring program it is important to consider the nature of the target population. Research conducted to date indicates that some populations adapt to home detention better than others. For example, one study indicated that offenders convicted of driving while intoxicated performed better than other offenders. Another study found that pretrial clients were significantly more likely to abscond from the program than were convicted offenders. It appears that program performance varies with the target population.

Finally, there is some evidence that the rehabilitative potential of electronic monitoring programs has been masked by the emphasis on surveillance and control. Home confinement can help stabilize an offender's life-style, and with an alcohol prohibition, control alcohol (and possibly drug) problems. In addition, the constraints of staying at home appear to encourage employment. Many offenders report improved job performance and domestic relations while in the programs.

Electronically monitored home confinement at this point in its development appears to be a viable intermediate sanction, but not a panacea for all of our correctional problems. Properly delivered to an appropriate population, electronically monitored home detention is moderately punitive and offers rehabilitative potential.

Electronic Monitoring in Marion County, Indiana

Michael G. Maxfield and Terry L. Baumer

Electronically monitored (EM) home detention programs have been under study in Marion County (Indianapolis), Indiana, since 1986. Three evaluations sponsored by the National Institute of Justice have examined EM programs for convicted adults, adjudicated juveniles, and adults awaiting disposition of criminal charges. The first two were designed as randomized experiments, while the pretrial evaluation was a detailed case study. The county community corrections agency administered both adult programs; the juvenile court implemented juvenile EM. Results concerning use of EM as an alternative sanction or a pretrial disposition are mixed.

All three evaluations were conducted by researchers from Indiana University, with unequivocal support from county justice officials. Each study collected data on program operations, criminal records, new arrests of program clients, and records of computer-generated calls to those on EM. There were two additional sources of information for convicted adults and juveniles: one-year follow-up criminal histories, and client interviews at program intake and at completion.

EVALUATION AND PROGRAM DESCRIPTIONS

The program for convicted adults randomly assigned persons to one of two methods of monitoring: manual telephone and field contacts, or an electronic programmed contact system. In either case, offenders received a suspended sentence and home detention as a condition of probation. Although targeted at all adults convicted of nonviolent offenses for which sentences could be suspended, 64 percent of those in the study were sentenced for felony charges of driving while intoxicated (DWI).

Evaluation of a program targeting juvenile burglars was begun in 1989 and is still in progress; preliminary findings are discussed here. Juveniles initially charged with burglary and convicted of either burglary or theft were program targets. Clients were randomly assigned to one of four home detention treatments: manual contact only; electronic programmed contact; home visits by police; and both police visits and EM.

Defendants awaiting disposition in jail were considered for the pretrial program if they faced misdemeanor or certain nonviolent felony charges and were not eligible for other forms of pretrial release. Those who met additional eligibility criteria (living arrangements, criminal history) were assigned to a programmed contact system identical to that used for convicted adults and juveniles.

HIGHLIGHTS OF FINDINGS

Three types of program exits were possible: successful release from EM, termination due to rule violations, and absconding. Among convicted adults, 81 percent were "successfuls," while 5 percent absconded and 14 percent were removed for rule violations. Fewer pretrial clients were successfully released (73 percent), 14 percent absconded, and 13 percent violated. According to preliminary data, the juvenile court classified 99 percent of its clients as successful exits.

However, on other measures of program performance, juvenile burglars performed substantially less well: 11 percent were rearrested while on home detention, compared with 5 percent for convicted adults and 1 percent for pretrial defendants. Only 17 percent of computer-generated calls to juveniles produced a successful electronic contact, compared with just over 50 percent for each adult program.

Discrepancies between agency definitions of successful program completion and more objective indicators of client performance warrant some comment. Observation of day-to-day program operations revealed that, compared with the adult program, the juvenile court and cooperating agencies paid less attention to delivering program elements and using information from arrest records and the EM equipment. Staff were less well trained in operating electronic equipment, and police visits were inconsistent. These findings also underscore the limits of relying on agency definitions of program outcomes. Even though virtually all juvenile burglars were classified as successfully completing home detention, less subjective performance measures point to more official records of misconduct (arrests) and fewer successful electronic contacts. A related point is that tolerance of misbehavior can produce self-defined success, while stricter monitoring and enforcement at least potentially increase program failures. Program failures exacerbate facility crowding when offenders are returned to jail.

Home detention may seem like easy time to the general public, potentially undermining political support for EM. But exit interviews revealed that life on home detention was rated hard or very hard by 44 percent of convicted adults who were electronically monitored. One result of this perceived hardship was that persons on EM worked more. Since being on the job was the only legitimate reason for extended absence from home, many clients sought overtime work or obtained second jobs to get out of the house. Family members of EM clients suffered side effects from late-night calls: 78 percent of adult offenders on EM reported complaints from family members, compared to 49 percent from the families of those on manual monitoring.

One year after release from home detention, 37 percent of the postconviction clients had been arrested for a new offense or charged with a warrant or probation violation. About half of new arrests occurred within four months of release (17 percent within 30 days), suggesting that postrelease adjustment may be difficult. Perhaps most significant, the large number of DWI clients were less likely than other clients to be arrested for new offenses in the one-year follow-up.

Compared with convicted offenders, fewer pretrial clients completed the program successfully, and failures were more often the result of absconding. Absconders tended to have the most extensive criminal histories compared with other program exits. The differing incentives faced by convicted offenders and those awaiting trial help explain higher absconding rates by the latter. Convicted offenders are serving a sentence at home and see greater freedom on the horizon if they comply with program requirements. In contrast, if pretrial clients are convicted of pending charges (81 percent were), time in jail or prison may be in the offing. The possibility of less freedom in the future may create incentives for pretrial clients to "live it up" or flee before their cases are adjudicated.

Household living arrangements were also related to client success in the pretrial program. The relatively small number of married clients who lived with their spouses had the highest success rate; 92 percent were released to court. Most clients were single and lived with various family members or acquaintances. Among this group, those living with parents or opposite-sex roommates fared best. Clients who lived with other relatives or same-sex roommates were riskier bets, with 60 percent successfully completing the program.

CONCLUSIONS

The somewhat different results from evaluations of these three programs in Marion County provide some guidance for the use of EM elsewhere.

First, home detention with EM is not equally suitable for all types of persons who might otherwise be incarcerated or subject to some other sanction. People who have long criminal records exhibit a pattern of unlawful behavior that is not consistent with expectations that they will remain at home and behave themselves. This is especially true for persons awaiting trial. People who have stronger or more recent family ties and those in marital or quasi-marital relationships perform better than persons with less structured living arrangements.

Second, EM equipment is continually evolving, but remains anything but foolproof. Technical and basic design problems remain and account for a large proportion of unsuccessful attempts to contact a client. Innovative equipment should be approached with extreme caution. Marion County abandoned a voiceprint verification system after two weeks of trials when computer software was unable to distinguish male and female voices. Even relatively well-established systems are not easily modified and require diligent staff attention.

Finally, it is crucial to recognize that EM is not a magic bullet. At its best, EM supplements traditional probation services. Electronic contacts supplement but cannot replace staff contacts. Records of computer contacts must be viewed as an additional source of information about client behavior. Recognition of these limits, together with careful implementation of EM systems, are crucial components of their success. The Marion County juvenile burglar evaluation illustrates that inconsistent implementation and lack of organizational commitment undermine the effectiveness of electronic monitoring. Experience with the pretrial program underscores this lesson. Although absconding was more common, compared to both postconviction programs, this problem was reduced as community corrections staff gained experience.

Electronic Monitoring in the U.S.
J. Robert Lilly

Since renewed scholarly, practical, and commercial interest in electronic monitoring developed in the early 1980s, it has been a "growth industry" for all concerned. It has yet, however, to live up to the hopes of its boosters, nor have the worst fears of skeptics been realized. To the contrary, vigorous debates about electronic monitoring (EM) have given way to sophisticated evaluation studies while EM has increasingly become institutionalized.

EXPANSION

There are no accurate current national data on EM, but informed estimates for the last two years report between 50,000 and 70,000 people monitored per day in the United States. The annual doubling of use in the late 1980s has ended. Modest but steady growth is found in established programs. At least eight states are attempting to reduce prison costs by reducing sentence lengths for some offenses and reclassifying others so that offenders can be supervised by intermediate sanctions including EM. All states have had at least one EM program since 1990. Approximately 1,800 federal offenders are now being monitored, which leaves room for substantial expansion.

IMPACT

Research on EM's impact has focused primarily on budgets, overcrowding, and equipment problems. States, including Michigan, Florida, and Illinois, and county and city governments have reported significant savings and reductions in prison or jail overcrowding. No report that I have seen, however, indicates a budget or appropriation reduction for corrections because of savings derived from EM. More typical are claims that incarceration costs would have been much higher had EM not been available. Reports comparing or evaluating EM on criteria other than cost and overcrowding are uncommon; exceptions are found in Baumer et al. (1993) and Lilly et al. (1993).

TECHNOLOGY

Other than the creation of "drive-by" systems, there have been no major technological developments in the last few years comparable to the mid-1980s refinements of passive and active EM equipment. Drive-by systems allow probation and parole supervisors to determine from an automobile whether monitorees are where they are supposed to be. Industry research and development continues to focus on equipment refinements including size and efficiency.

Software research related to EM has included a number of improvements that reduce paperwork demands on supervisors while increasing the accountability of monitorees, usually without additional cost to agencies. B.I. Inc. and Digital Products have made software available for automated 900 phone calls that allow probationers and parolees to update their files without a face-to-face meeting with supervisors. Similar but enhanced software allows monitorees to report to their supervisors by phone. Phone companies send the collected fees to EM vendors, who usually forward them at no cost to supervising agencies. The 900 phone charges and fees are paid by monitorees.

NET-WIDENING

One of the greatest concerns about EM in the 1980s was that it would be so easy to implement that judges would use it in the manner of the proverbial child with a hammer, hitting everything and everybody within reach. This was a serious concern and should continue to be, coupled as EM is to the Orwellian "new age of surveillance" and its capacity to compromise privacy. While I am not able to address this issue fully here, there are some grounds for believing the Orwellian fears may be exaggerated. A seven-year study of EM and its use for offenders convicted of driving while intoxicated (DWI) was done at Pride, Inc., West Palm Beach, Florida. EM was applied to less than 2 percent of those arrested for DWI, and there was no evidence of net-widening. EM was generally not used as an alternative to conventional probation, but in lieu of jail (Lilly et al. 1993).

VENDOR DEVELOPMENTS

The relatively low number of persons monitored nationally, low daily monitoring fees, and stiff competition among vendors have kept equipment costs low and prevented significant vendor profit. Competition within the monitoring market recently changed when one of the leading vendors, Corrections Services Incorporated, settled a lawsuit with its equipment provider, Marconi of the United Kingdom. If Corrections Services withdraws from monitoring, competition may decrease—and profits increase—among the remaining vendors.

MEDIA COVERAGE

Throughout most of the 1980s, nearly 2,500 EM-related newspaper articles appeared per year. EM received extensive media attention, most of which addressed concern about loss of privacy, new programs, evaluations, and the high expectations of criminal-justice officials. By the late 1980s and early 1990s, media coverage shifted to focus on program deficiencies and offenses committed by monitored offenders.

COMMERCIAL CORRECTIONS COMPLEX

Corrections in the U.S. represents at least a $65-billion industry and EM is only its newest component. It will continue to be implemented in the United States and elsewhere and increasingly to attract the commercial interest of numerous parties, not the least of which are security corporations whose markets already range from military installations to home burglar alarms. For practitioners and others concerned with jail and prison overcrowding, EM remains an underused alternative. It is doubtful, however, whether it will ever successfully counter our capacity to incarcerate.

Electronic Monitoring in England and Wales
George Mair

Electronic monitoring is not now in use in England and Wales despite government interest dating from 1987, pilot projects launched and evaluated in 1989–1990, and passage of legislation in 1991 establishing electronic monitoring of offenders on curfew as an authorized sanction.

The same claims were made for electronic monitoring (EM) in England and Wales as in the United States. It would act as a real alternative to custody, it would give probation some much-needed bite, it was very cheap, and it would aid rehabilitation.

The claims for EM were received very differently in the two countries. In England and Wales, a deliberate four-year process of planning and evaluation was started. In the United States, electronic monitoring schemes were hurriedly introduced in scores of sites by beleaguered criminal justice professionals. Between 1986 and 1990 the growth of EM was astonishing: a daily monitored population of 95 in 1986 grew to more than 12,000 in 1990, and the number of states using electronic monitoring rose from seven to fifty (Renzema 1992). Whatever the bases for the widespread adoption of EM, it was certainly not based on hard evaluation evidence. Little evaluation preceded widespread implementation, and the bulk of the early studies were simplistic and produced equivocal results.

In England and Wales (it should be emphasized that electronic monitoring did not take place in Scotland or Northern Ireland) the approach to EM was rather different. Here, a pilot project was set up and evaluated during 1989–1990, and the electronic monitoring of offenders on curfew orders was introduced as a new community penalty in the Criminal Justice Act 1991 but has not been implemented. EM has not been used since the end of the pilot projects in April 1990. So what happened?

THE PILOT PROJECTS

By 1987 electronic monitoring was on the policy agenda in England and Wales. By mid-1988 a decision had been made to set up an experimental project and to have it evaluated by the Home Office Research and Planning Unit. Unusually, the researchers were involved from the very beginning. The researchers were members of the Home Office Steering Group, which oversaw the pilots and also served as members of the local liaison committees.

The EM pilots suffered from several major limitations. First, while the idea was to look at EM as a possible tool for monitoring a curfew order (in other words, as part of a court sentence for a convicted offender), existing legislation would not permit this. Passage of enabling legislation on such short notice was not feasible; the pilots were therefore confined to unconvicted defendants, and EM was used as a bail condition.

Second, because of budgetary constraints the projects were confined to three areas for only six months each—not a long time for such a major innovation to be given a chance to settle down.

Third, EM was by no means a "neutral" innovation, and many of those involved in the projects had fairly fixed views about it prior to the starting date. Fourth, the bail/jail decision can involve all of the major agencies in the criminal-justice system: the police, the Crown Prosecution Service, the courts, the probation service, and the prison service. Coordinating all of these in such a short time was a near-impossible task. Finally, control exercised by the Home Office over the pilot projects led to serious methodological problems for the evaluation (Mair and Nee 1990).

After twelve months of hard work the first project began in

Nottingham City in August 1989, the second a month later in North Tyneside, and the third in October in Tower Bridge in London. Each ran for six months, although a few more weeks were needed for the courts to deal with those who were monitored. The target group were defendants who, in the absence of EM, would have been detained in custody. They had to be volunteers, seventeen or older, residing in the area covered by the jurisdiction of the court, and not likely to pose a danger to the public or cause any undue hardship to their families if monitoring took place at home.

THE RESULTS

Despite (or perhaps because of) the publicity surrounding the projects and the amount of local planning and discussion that had taken place, only 50 defendants, all male, were placed on electronic monitoring; 17 in Nottingham, 15 in North Tyneside, and 18 at Tower Bridge. Of those monitored, 19 were aged between seventeen and twenty, 15 were between twenty-one and twenty-five, and the remaining 16 were between twenty-six and forty-seven. As almost all had previously been detained in custody and the remainder had been held overnight by the police, it is reasonable to assume that EM was used as an alternative to confinement in all cases.

Courts were able to monitor defendants for up to twenty-four hours per day, and two defendants—both in Nottingham—had such a curfew. Most curfews were for sixteen or more hours per day (28 of 50). Of defendants monitored, 29 absconded or were charged with a new offense. In total there were 217 alleged time violations, the majority (63 percent) for periods of less than thirty minutes.

Interviews with twenty of the fifty defendants suggested that EM was not seen as an easy option. It was considered to be restrictive and much closer to confinement in jail than to bail with conditions, but the advantages of being at home with one's family outweighed the restrictions. Long curfews were viewed as particularly oppressive, and the possibility of domestic problems was acknowledged.

Neither the police nor sentencers had a great deal of confidence in EM—at least as far as the pilot projects were concerned. For the police, public safety was a key issue, and they did not feel comfortable with their role in creating the projects. They were expected initially to identify cases in which bail should be opposed but then to assess this group to decide whether any could be released subject to EM.

Magistrates and judges were dubious about the applicability of EM as an alternative to custody and expressed skepticism about the reliability of the technology. They felt that it was very difficult to find defendants who were appropriate for EM; this was a critical factor in the low numbers who were monitored during the pilot projects. EM was considered to be suitable for mature, responsible people with a family and employment, but these were not characteristics associated with those monitored during the pilot projects; they tended to be young and unemployed, and many may have lacked the self-discipline necessary to cope with EM's demands.

AFTERMATH

Given the short time-scale, the low numbers monitored, that procedures had to be amended in the light of practice, and that the projects could not evaluate the use of EM as an adjunct to a sentence, it was always going to be difficult to draw clear conclusions from the evaluation. It was evident, however, that EM was feasible as a surveillance tool. The only major drawback to a national system of electronic monitoring appeared to be the costs of setting it up. Use of EM as a means of monitoring a curfew order was authorized in the Criminal Justice Act 1991: curfew orders could not be made for longer than six months, or monitoring for less than two hours or more than twelve in any one day.

Most of the new powers created in the Act were implemented on October 1, 1992, but the power to impose a curfew order remains in limbo. This cannot be seen as an example of policy being shaped by research: the evaluation did not show EM to be a great success, but neither did it demonstrate such a degree of failure that EM was summarily abandoned.

Two closely linked reasons explain the lack of progress on EM. First, budgetary constraints meant that adequate funding was not available. Second, while the new Act meant that curfew orders would have to be introduced on a national basis, electronic monitoring could be introduced on an area-by-area basis. Given financial constraints, this might have been an advantage; but taking account of the need to gain the confidence of the courts in the new curfew order, this was a drawback. Arrangements would have to be made for monitoring the curfew order in the absence of EM. But to introduce curfew orders that were not monitored by EM would be difficult, as complex negotiations would be necessary to decide what agency would carry out enforcement; no existing agency was keen to take this on, and setting up a new agency was not an easy option. Because EM could not be introduced on a national basis, the curfew order was put on ice with the understanding that it would be considered again as the workings of the new Act were reviewed.

The evaluation of the pilot projects showed that EM is not a quick and easy answer to penal problems, but it is primarily because of lack of money that EM is not currently in use as a criminal-justice tool in England and Wales. This, of course, is ironic, as one of the great claims made for EM is that it saves money (a claim as yet unsubstantiated by hard evidence). The use of electronic monitoring for offenders may yet be resuscitated; it certainly has not disappeared from the penal agenda, and with the likelihood of a criminal justice bill within the next year or so it may make a reappearance.

4

PARTIAL
AND
SHORT-TERM
CONFINEMENT

Introduction

Boot camps are what is new. Partial confinement has long been in use in a variety of forms—halfway houses, ad hoc sentences to nighttime and weekend confinement, and partial home detention by means of curfew conditions to probation and parole orders. Day-reporting centers, though in form a recent innovation in the United States, are in substance little more than a systematic approach to previous ad hoc use of partial confinement.

Boot camps are the most recent of the newly popular "intermediate" sanctions. Intermediate is in quotation marks because one might reasonably wonder why a 90-to-180-day stay in prison is not regarded as a prison sentence. The standard explanation is that boot camps are often used in lieu of longer conventional prison sentences and accordingly that they are alternatives to longer terms of incarceration. Or, they could be considered part of a continuum of sanctions that not only extends between prison and probation but also includes gradations within prison sentences. Both of these are plausible reasons for inclusion of materials on boot camps in a book on intermediate sanctions, although they apply only to a subset of boot camps.

Like most intermediate sanctions, boot camps come in a variety of forms, including the customary contrast between back- and front-end programs. In New York State, for example, offenders are placed in boot camp programs by corrections officials, and successful completion of the boot camp results in substantially earlier release from prison. Because participants are selected from prison and are released early, programs such as New York's are likely to save corrections beds and costs.

In many boot camp programs, however, as in most house arrest and intensive supervision programs, "prison-bound" offenders are sentenced directly to the boot camp by judges. This inevitably raises the problems that bedevil most front-end programs. Judges may, whatever the official policy of the boot camp operators, use them for offenders to whom a less restrictive sanction would otherwise have been applied. When a third to half of those assigned to the boot camp fail to complete the program, their penalties are then ratcheted up again to regular imprisonment. Dale Parent's article demonstrates that boot camps are likely to be cost-effective only if net-widening is kept to very low levels. As a result, only back-end programs are likely in the end to have a reasonable chance of saving taxpayers' money.

Boot camps vary widely in their content. In most states, including Georgia and Alabama, boot camp programming consists largely of military drills, strict discipline, exercise, and physical labor. In a few states, of which New York is the most active, boot camp programming includes drill and exercise, but the program emphasis is at least equally on drug treatment, education, and vocational training.

Boot camps are at an early stage of the normal cycle for intermediate sanctions. Most corrections officials do not support establishment of boot camps, primarily for reasons discussed in the following paragraphs. They remain popular, however, with elected officials who want to demonstrate their toughness. This is why proposals have been made, including some by President Bill Clinton, for boot camps for nonviolent first offenders. This makes little policy sense. Many first offenders are never arrested again. Most will not otherwise be prison-bound, but many will fail in the boot camp and wind up serving significant prison terms. Many are likely to be socialized into deviance by others in the boot camp or later in prison, and for many, their chances of achieving law-abiding conventional lives will be reduced. Such programs cannot reduce corrections costs, and, as emerging evaluation findings instruct, they are no more effective at reducing recidivism than are other sanctions.

The article by Doris MacKenzie summarizes the findings from the first major national effort to establish the effects of boot camps. Two findings stand out. First, psychologists using psychometric measures have several times found measurable increases in self-esteem of offenders who complete boot camp requirements. Second, however—as is found in most correctional evaluations—successful program completion has no significant effect on recidivism rates.

Corrections officials have no difficulty reconciling those findings. Many tell anecdotes of former prisoners who, when released from the boot camp, appeared to feel good about themselves and to want to stay out of trouble, but who, six months later, were no better off than before they entered the program. Why? Because the graduates returned to the neighborhoods and influences that led them into trouble initially, and because the problems of poverty, broken families, inadequate education and work skills, and unemployment were no less difficult for them after the boot camp than before.

Less need be said about partial confinement. Halfway houses have long served as way stations between prison and freedom, programs that provided a transition back into normal life. Clients have traditionally been expected to go to work or school during the day and to live in the halfway house at night. Sometimes halfway houses are "halfway in" rather than "halfway out" and are expected to place controls short of imprisonment on offenders for whom probation appears insufficiently restrictive.

Partial confinement in jails or halfway houses has long been used as a sanction for offenders who have committed moderately serious crimes but who are employed or employable. The objective is to achieve the punitive effect of incarceration while allowing the offender to continue to work to support himself and his family.

Day-reporting centers in the United States are mostly used as "halfway out programs," with the twist that offenders stay in their own homes at night and spend their days at the center. The first centers were consciously patterned after day-reporting centers in England; these, as the article by George Mair relates, are less punitive than American programs and provide a fuller array of services. Day-reporting centers, as the articles by John Larivee and Dale Parent indicate, have not as yet been as widely adopted in the United States as other intermediate sanctions, and have not yet been the subjects of serious evaluations.

Day-Reporting Centers

Day-Reporting Centers
Dale G. Parent

After he was denied pretrial release, Frank faced several months in jail awaiting trial. But staff from the Connecticut Prison Association reviewed his case and recommended that the judge release him to its Alternative Incarceration Center (AIC) in Hartford. The judge agreed; he ordered Frank to report to the AIC office every morning and to file an itinerary showing where he would be, and how he could be contacted, for each hour of each day. The judge ordered Frank to look for a job (Frank used the association's employment project to find a job as a custodian at a local factory) and to attend drug-use counseling sessions at the AIC. Finally, the judge ordered Frank to submit to random drug-use tests.

The Hartford AIC is one of eight privately run day-reporting centers funded by the Connecticut Department of Corrections that are designed to reduce jail and prison crowding. Connecticut's AICs recruit persons denied pretrial release, sentenced offenders who otherwise would be imprisoned, and prison inmates eligible for supervised home release, a type of furlough.

Day-reporting centers (DRCs) are a new intermediate sanction that combines high levels of surveillance and extensive services, treatments, or activities. DRCs have roots in both juvenile day-treatment programs, in which delinquents attend classes or undergo treatment at a special facility during the day but live at home; and British day centers, which provide "day care" and treatment for chronic, but minor, offenders who are unemployable. Although a few isolated programs existed earlier, most American DRCs opened after 1985. A

1989 study by the National Institute of Justice (NIJ) located 22 day-reporting centers in eight states, with most in Connecticut (8), Massachusetts (5), Minnesota (3), and Wisconsin (2).

While DRCs provide more intensive supervision and services than offenders otherwise would get, existing programs vary greatly. No dominant program model has emerged. Most were created to reduce prison and jail crowding, but a few were established to treat offenders with special problems (e.g., abused, drug-using females). Some are surveillance oriented, while others emphasize both treatment and support. Some recruit offenders at sentencing, others take prisoners released early from jail or prison, and some—as in Connecticut—recruit from several sources. Some states used DRCs in lieu of imprisonment for probation or parole violators. Some DRCs provide structured aftercare following a short residential placement. DRCs' average duration of supervision varies from forty days to nine months.

At the time of the NIJ study, DRCs existed in states that did not operate intensive supervision programs (ISPs). Except for three programs run by Massachusetts sheriffs, all were privately operated. A few had super-intensive contact standards—in Massachusetts contacts ranged from forty to eighty per week. However, just as with ISP, contact standards varied widely. Generally, DRC staff made fewer contacts in the field than ISP officers and relied more on office and telephone contacts. Hence, caseloads per staff member tended to be somewhat higher than those found in most ISP programs. That, coupled with the lower pay scale typically found in private-sector programs, suggests that day reporting may be a cheaper way to provide high-contact supervision. However, no solid cost analyses have been done.

DRCs may benefit correctional agencies struggling to reduce crowding or to comply with court-ordered population caps. For example, it may be quicker to expand releasing capacity by contracting with private vendors who are not bound by public personnel rules or union contracts. In Minnesota, neighborhood opposition kept private agencies from expanding residential facilities for prison work release placement. Nonetheless, Minnesota's DOC doubled its annual prison work release capacity by cutting residential work release from 120 to 60 days and adding a 60-day day-reporting period, during which graduates report to the residences for surveillance and programming but live in their own homes. Because most work releasees who wash out of the program fail during the first few weeks (while they are in the residential phase), Minnesota found that 97 percent of participants complete the program satisfactorily.

At the time of the NIJ study, no outcome evaluations had been done, and consequently there were no data indicating whether offenders succeed at higher or lower rates in day reporting than in other available placements. The NIJ study noted, however, that completion rates in day reporting varied considerably and seemed to be related to characteristics of clients recruited into the programs. Minnesota's very high completion rate may be affected by a two-level "creaming" process: only better-risk prison inmates get accepted for work release, and of those, only the best-risk cases complete the residential period and enter day reporting. In DRCs that accept general population inmates released early from prisons and jails, about two thirds to three fourths of those admitted successfully complete day reporting. In DRCs that recruit probation or parole violators, completion rates typically are lower—ranging from 30 to 60 percent.

If policymakers want DRCs to reduce prison and jail crowding, they should use day reporting as an early release mechanism and should let corrections officials (not judges at the time of sentencing) select inmates for DRC placement. Among inmates released early, DRCs should be used for those who pose the greatest risk to the public or who have the most serious problems that are likely to impair their adjustment. To reduce total costs, officials should use less structured and less expensive forms of supervision for low-risk, low-need inmates who are granted early release. Future research should focus on DRC's costs and impacts on offenders' adjustments.

Day Reporting in Massachusetts
John J. Larivee

In October 1986, the sheriff of Hampden County opened the first day-reporting center (DRC). One year later, the Crime and Justice Foundation opened the Metropolitan Day Reporting Center in Boston. Day-reporting centers today serve eight counties and the state department of correction.

What is a day-reporting center?

It is a nonresidential program providing intensive supervision to an offender population that would otherwise be incarcerated.

In Massachusetts, the clients are, for the most part, inmates serving up to two and one half years in a county jail who are within three months of parole or discharge. The inmates live at home while remaining under the jurisdiction of the correctional administrator.

The offender reports to the center seven days a week and completes an itinerary of activities for the next twenty-four hours. The itinerary, prepared with a case manager, identifies where the inmate will be and when and how he or she will travel from place to place.

The offender is in telephone contact with program staff at least twice each day and is randomly tested for drug and alcohol use at least twice a week. In addition, staff periodically visit the client at home or at some other community location.

While in the program, the inmate must either be employed or in school and regularly participate in a treatment program, especially during evenings and weekends. Each offender contributes at least four hours per week to a community service assignment and adheres to a curfew.

How was this concept sold in Willie Horton's state?

In two words, very deliberately. In 1984, the Crime and Justice Foundation, a century-old nonprofit criminal-justice agency based in Boston, launched an effort to develop a correctional option that could safely manage in the community offenders who would otherwise go to jail.

The first step was to learn from the successes and failures of others. We examined community-based programs, reviewed evaluations on sentencing alternatives, and communicated with people operating programs.

We learned of the day centers operated by the Probation Service of England and Wales and became convinced that the concept had potential for local adoption.

We were also convinced that our objective of managing inmates in the community would not meet with tremendous favor.

Our first task, therefore, was to gain public officials' confidence, which required attention to political and professional realities. We pursued broad understanding and support; we convened a committee of advisors, disseminated briefing papers, conferred with criminal-justice executives, and cooperated with related efforts such as the Governor's Special Commission on Correctional Alternatives.

After several months, the idea of the day-reporting center took on a life of its own. It became a correctional option accepted by people of diverse political and professional perspectives. That acceptance provided individual correctional administrators the political confidence to go forward.

What guided the design of this community corrections program?

Early in 1986, the Crime and Justice Foundation began working with the Hampden County Sheriff's Department to design a day-reporting center. That work was guided by three considerations: such a program must work to achieve public safety through supervision; it must hold the offender accountable for his behavior through use of sanctions; and it must provide the resources for the offender to deal with addiction, unemployment, lack of education, and other problems through treatment.

These themes are important for any community-based option. Depending, however, on the particular goals, political environment, target population, and location of the community-based option, the intensity of each theme would vary—more or less supervision, sanction, and treatment.

We also recognized the need to guard against the "more is better" syndrome—the belief that more supervision, sanctions, and services make for a better program. We feared that this would result in an overly expensive, overly rigid program that no offender could successfully complete and no agency could properly deliver. Thus, careful attention was given to ensure that the operational components were necessary but not excessive.

What have been the results and accomplishments?

The major metropolitan areas of Massachusetts—Boston, Springfield, and Worcester—operate DRCs that serve the local county jails. These facilities combined hold 60 percent of the county inmate population in Massachusetts.

An evaluation of the Hampden County center found that 81 percent of the first ninety-six clients to complete the program did so successfully, 18 percent were terminated early for violating the program's terms (drug use or curfew violation), and 1 percent was arrested for a new crime. The study concluded that the program was "successfully managing the transition to the community of otherwise incarcerated offenders"; was "effectively supervising offenders in the community"; and was "directly impacting overcrowding" (Center for Applied Social Research 1988).

A survey of four centers found that over two thirds of the first 700 participants successfully completed the programs. Of the one third who were terminated, most were for substance abuse and only seventeen (2.4 percent) had new arrests. A later examination of the same centers reported a successful completion rate of 78 percent, with 20 percent returned to jail for program violations and only 2 percent failures for new crime or escape (Curtin and McDevitt 1990).

The Crime and Justice Foundation's Metropolitan Day Reporting Center has realized similar results. Of the first 433 clients to complete the program, 67 percent did so successfully, 30 percent were terminated for program violations, and 3 percent were arrested for a new offense or escape.

It is essential that the centers operate consistently with their original goals. The centers are achieving 100 percent success at maintaining a caseload of diverted jail-bound offenders. Every client in a DRC would otherwise be incarcerated; additionally, no client is kept in the center longer than he or she would be kept in jail. The centers are achieving 97 percent success at managing offenders in the community safely and effectively. Only 3 percent fail owing to an arrest for a new crime or escape, and none so far for a violent offense.

Whether used as an initial sanction for first-time offenders, as a last chance prior to incarceration, or as an early release mechanism, implementation of day centers must be purposeful and planned. Their design must incorporate activities aimed at providing supervision, sanction, and treatment. Their intensity must be based on the needs of the offender population, criminal justice system, and local community.

Day Centers in England and Wales
George Mair

The probation center was the penal success story of the eighties in England and Wales (originally known as day centers, they have been renamed under the provisions of the Criminal Justice Act 1991). Probation centers have played a key role in moving probation center-stage in England and Wales, and they are increasingly being established in the United States, where they tend to be referred to as day-reporting centers.

Probation centers are typically used as diversion from incarceration for offenders who are young, male, unemployed, and convicted of property crimes, who have several previous convictions and have previously been in custody. Attendance orders run from thirty to sixty days and require regular attendance at the center for therapeutic, vocational, medical (including substance abuse), and other programs. Especially in light of the high reoffending risks presented by their clients, the centers are widely regarded as successful.

ORIGINS

Seeds for the centers were sown in the sixties with two unrelated developments. First, there were renewed anxieties about the rising prison population and conditions inside prisons. Second, there was a disenchantment among some probation officers with the traditional style of individual casework and a corresponding interest in group work with offenders. Recognizing these developments, the 1972 Criminal Justice Act introduced day-training centers aimed at diverting from custodial sentences the older, petty persistent offenders whose offending seemed to stem from social inadequacy, and subjecting them to intensive, structured training. Only four day-training centers were ever set up, and they did not flourish (low referral rates, relatively high costs, lack of flexibility, and the introduction of community service orders at the same time did not help the new centers).

Many probation officers at the same time were setting up day centers that had no statutory basis and that catered to various types of offenders and nonoffenders. Some offenders were ordered by the courts to attend these day centers, but as there was no legal basis for this, the practice was ruled unlawful in 1981. By this time, it had been decided to repeal the day-training center legislation, and thus there would be no way to require offenders to attend a day center. However, legislation soon passed providing that during a probation order an offender could be required to attend a day center for up to sixty days; such centers had to be approved by the local probation committee.

By the middle of 1985 there were more than eighty probation centers in England and Wales, albeit not equally distributed. For example, in Somerset, a predominantly rural county, there were five centers, while in Middlesex, which covers a large part of London, there were none. Although probation centers were encouraged by the government, probation services were under no obligation to set them up. Some chief probation officers opposed them because they believed high-risk offenders could be dealt with without having a costly day center. A minority of probation officers did not agree with the idea of requiring offenders to attend centers—they preferred voluntary attendance. In 1985, a total of 1,800 offenders were required to attend a probation center; by 1991 this figure had grown by more than 66 percent to 3,000.

PROBATION CENTERS IN OPERATION

It would be misleading to talk of a "typical" probation center. Some restrict themselves to offenders ordered to attend. Others accept those with other requirements or offenders with straight probation orders who attend voluntarily. In some cases centers have been forced to widen their target group as a result of low referral rates or pressure from the courts. A few centers use the center building as the focus of all work by the probation team; thus, the center is used for normal probation supervision, as a base for community service, and for after-care of released prisoners and parole supervision.

The number and kind of staff vary: probation officers both full- and part-time, probation ancillary workers, volunteers, sessional supervisors, and clerical staff may all be employed. The kind of worker tends to reflect the center's style and approach; very crudely, the greater the proportion of probation officers, the greater the emphasis on aspects of social work. The number of offenders dealt with at any one time varies—some centers can accept only about ten offenders, while others will take fifty or more (one critical factor is the size of the building available; another is the center's "philosophy"). The length of the order offered to the court and the opening times of centers also vary widely. Thus, while the maximum order is sixty days, the centers set their own programs and may offer only a thirty-day or forty-five-day program. Some centers open only for three or four half-days each week, some for two or three full days, some for four full days. Thus, a day-center order can mean very different things in different parts of the country: a thirty-day order where the center opens for three half-days of four hours each week is likely to be much less demanding than a sixty-day order where the center is open for four days, eight hours each day, every week.

The general approach is fairly pragmatic, but some centers emphasize control much more than others, and some are based on the principles of a therapeutic community. Most offer a wide range of activities for offenders, typically focused around four main elements: social/life skills (including confronting behavior, which is a key feature of all centers); art/craft classes (painting, woodwork, music, etc.); health/welfare activities (advice and help with substance abuse, claiming welfare, etc.); and sport. Many of the activities are compulsory, although offenders are usually permitted to exercise some choice in the more optional classes.

WHO ATTENDS?

A national survey of centers a few years ago (Mair 1988) found that most centers unequivocally saw their aim as diversion from custody. However, only 60 percent of those attending centers were there as a result of a court order. Most of those ordered to attend were male (95 percent) and unemployed (more than 80 percent). Those who ran centers were very much aware of the lack of female offenders: some thought few females fell into the center's target group; some felt that they were not being referred by field probation staff; some had tried to run their centers with a few female offenders, but had encountered problems in an atmosphere dominated by young, macho males.

Almost half of those ordered to attend were under twenty-one (45 percent) and a further 28 percent were between twenty-one and twenty-five. Sixty-six percent had been convicted of burglary or theft, while a further 15 percent had been convicted of car theft or motoring offenses. Only 2 percent had no previous convictions, while almost half (47 percent) had six or more. More than half had experienced custody (56 percent) and almost one fifth (18 percent) had been subject to a probation or community service order. The major differences between those ordered to attend and those who attended voluntarily lay in their previous criminal history; those ordered were twice as likely to have served a custodial sentence and twice as likely to have six or more previous convictions.

The national survey's findings affected policy in three ways. First, the research indicated that the probation service could deal with serious offenders. This became important in subsequent policy planning that culminated in the Criminal Justice Act 1991, which emphasized the role of the probation service in dealing with high-risk offenders in the community. Second, the project demonstrated that group work was an effective way of working with offenders. Probation centers were not places of chaos and confusion where offenders did more or less as they pleased, but were generally well organized and controlled. And third, the research pointed clearly to inconsistencies in probation center work (a not uncommon criticism of probation work generally) and therefore played a part in the development of national standards for all aspects of probation work.

EFFECTIVENESS

In the immediate aftermath of the 1982 legislation, probation centers became the "flavor of the month" for many probation areas and were allowed to develop without any real guidance or control. Too many sprang up without clear thought being given to aims and objectives and how these might be realized in practice; with little consideration given to the relationship among clientele, staff, aims, organizational structure, premises, and activities; and without consideration of the inequities for offenders of providing centers with differing hours of opening, days of operation, and length of orders.

Many centers have worked through their initial uncertainties and provide programs that are welcomed by the courts. For the most part, probation centers operate smoothly as part of the local probation service. However, there can be difficulties of disengagement when an offender becomes over-dependent on the more rigorous supervision supplied in a probation center (possibly attending for four days a week) and has problems adapting to the lesser demands of normal probation supervision (perhaps seeing a probation officer for forty-five minutes once a month).

A key objective for probation centers is to divert offenders from custodial sentences, and centers appear to fulfill this role successfully. The profile of those ordered to attend centers suggests that they are offenders with a high risk of a custodial sentence. Targeting has, if anything, improved over time. In the early days, probation officers relied heavily on "gut feeling" as to whether an offender was at risk of custody. Since the late eighties more and more probation areas have been using risk prediction scales to improve their decision-making.

Another important criterion for measuring the effectiveness of a court sentence is the reconviction rate, although it is no longer seen as the sole criterion by which a sentence should be judged. Reconviction rates are a problematic measure in many ways (they do not measure reoffending, they are heavily dependent on police activity, what is the "correct" follow-up period, how useful is a simple dichotomous measure of success/failure depending on whether one is reconvicted, etc.), but they cannot be ignored. Recent research showed a two-year reconviction rate for probation centers of 63 percent (Mair and Nee 1992). On the face of it, this may look high, but the offenders targeted by centers represent a very high risk group in terms of probability of reconviction. Probation centers may be condemning themselves to what appears to be a high reconviction rate by successfully diverting offenders from custody, and this must be taken into consideration when interpreting the overall reconviction rate. Another important consideration is that the reconviction data do not differentiate between those who successfully complete their day center order and those who fail to complete it.

Perhaps more significant than the overall reconviction rate for probation centers is the rate for individual centers. Four centers had two-year reconviction rates under 45 percent, and five centers had rates of 75 percent or more. The differences may to some extent be attributable to differences in the kinds of offenders accepted by centers (high-rate centers were more likely to have offenders with previous experience of custody and with six or more previous convictions), but other factors may also be significant. The kind of staff used in centers, the activities offered, the overall atmosphere (usually dictated by the officer in charge)—all could have an impact.

The costs of probation centers vary considerably, but they are always more expensive than straight probation. They are usually cheaper—and certainly not more expensive—than custody. Thus, as long as the centers are diverting offenders from custody and not diverting them from other community penalties, they should be cost-effective.

CONCLUSIONS

Probation centers have become an important part of English probation. Their contribution in encouraging group work and demonstrating that it is a practicable approach to dealing with offenders cannot be underestimated. And, on the whole, the centers are effective; they are successful in diverting offenders from custody, and the reconviction rates associated with them are not unacceptable. The best centers can be flexible and innovative; a number of the intensive probation programs that were set up during 1990–1992 were based on centers.

Probation centers have proved their worth, but this does not mean that they can rest on their laurels. They face a challenge in the new "combination order," combining probation and community service—which was introduced in October 1992—that could move into the position occupied by centers as the most demanding and rigorous community penalty. Research into the combination order currently under way should provide information about how far this is happening. And further research is needed to investigate the differences among centers and how centers fit into the range of projects now offered by probation services, and to consider in further detail the effectiveness of centers; such a study is planned. The research will contribute to the policy process and should ensure that probation centers remain relevant to probation work during the 1990s.

2

Boot Camps

Boot Camps Failing to Achieve Goals
Dale G. Parent

Most boot camps do not reduce recidivism, do not reduce prison populations, and, overall, do not reduce costs. They may be able to do some or all of these things, but only under conditions that are seldom satisfied.

In recent years correctional leaders, policymakers, and the general public have had a love affair with boot camp prisons. Boot camps are in sync with calls for harsher punishment. They provide striking visual images that provoke visceral responses in members of the viewing public. For corrections officials, boot camps are a promising treatment modality, a means to reinvigorate jaded staff, and a new way to reduce prison populations. In 1986 only three states had prison boot camps. By recent count, there were more than forty boot camps in twenty-nine states. Some serve adults and some serve juveniles. Local, state, and federal governments and private organizations run boot camps.

When boot camps first won notice, some practitioners and researchers urged (in vain, as it turned out) that boot camp development be put on hold while evaluations of the early programs sought answers to tough questions. What are boot camps' goals? Do they achieve them? Are there unintended side effects? Do boot camps save money?

Those early evaluation results are in. The findings are sobering. They oblige responsible policymakers and corrections officials to rethink the goals of boot camps, whether we ought to develop them, and, if so, how they should be structured.

To determine whether boot camps "work," we first must

know what boot camps are supposed to do. Leaders of agencies that run them will say boot camps are supposed to reduce recidivism, reduce prison populations, or reduce both recidivism and prison populations.

Any of these goals, if attained, could be a sufficient reason for running prison boot camps. What is their track record?

REDUCING RECIDIVISM

There is no evidence that existing boot camps significantly affect graduates' recidivism rates. In the late 1980s some states began to evaluate their boot camps. The National Institute of Justice (NIJ) funded an evaluation of Louisiana's boot camp, and later supported a coordinated evaluation of boot camps in eight states. The states funded the evaluations, but NIJ provided a national coordinator, convened state researchers to develop a common design, and provided technical assistance on design implementation and data analysis.

The multistate evaluation identifies two broad findings. Compared with similar offenders who do not go to boot camps, participants' attitudes and behaviors are better while they are in boot camps; but once released, graduates' recidivism rates are not significantly different.

It is important to emphasize that these evaluations did not randomly assign eligible offenders to boot camps and other correctional programs. Instead, they compared boot camp participants and graduates with similar groups of offenders who received other sentences. Thus, we cannot conclusively say that boot camps have no significant impact on recidivism. However, the findings are similar across all the programs evaluated and provide converging evidence that boot camps, as they have been conceived, implemented, and operated, do not significantly affect postrelease criminality.

REDUCING PRISON POPULATIONS

Do boot camps reduce prison populations? As typically designed and used, boot camps are more likely to increase prison populations, crowding, and total correctional costs than to decrease them. Boot camps can cut prison populations only under a limited set of difficult-to-achieve conditions.

A boot camp simulation model developed at Abt Associates, Inc., estimates the impact of various boot camp design options on prison bed-space requirements. The model identifies points where officials make decisions whether offenders go to a boot camp or receive some other disposition; specifies the probability of each option being selected; specifies how long offenders will be confined under each option; and describes the percentage who fail to complete the boot camp, the percentage of graduates who return to prison, and the length of their reconfinement. Each time an option results in confinement, the model computes the total number of days of confinement and sums them across all options being tested.

To simulate the effects of different boot camp options on prison bed-space requirements, the model is run over and over, each time changing one option while holding all others constant, and recording, for each change, the total number of prison beds needed. For example, one set of runs might test the impact of different probabilities of imprisonment for boot camp admissions—that is, if the boot camp did not exist, what are the odds these offenders would get probation versus prison? A low probability (e.g., 10 or 20 percent) represents a design option in which most offenders sentenced to boot camp normally would get probation. This might typify a selection process in which judges directly sentence first-time offenders to boot camps. A high probability (90 or 100 percent) represents a design option in which those sentenced to boot camp face virtually certain imprisonment. This might typify a selection process in which the department of corrections picks boot camp participants from among incoming regular prison inmates. Other simulations might test the impact of different durations for the boot camp, different in-program and postrelease failure rates, etc. In the end, the impact of different design options is determined by comparing the total projected bed-space requirements each one produces.

The simulation model reveals that five factors are particularly important in determining boot camps' impact on prison bed-space needs:

(1) the probability that boot camp inmates would be imprisoned if the boot camp did not exist;

(2) the boot camp's annual capacity (which, in turn, is determined largely by the number of beds available, the number of offenders who fit boot camp eligibility criteria, the program's duration, and policies governing replacement of those who fail to complete the program);

(3) the in-program failure rate for those who enter the boot camp;

(4) the difference between offenders' regular prison terms and the duration of the boot camp program; and

(5) the return-to-prison rate for boot camp graduates after their return to community supervision (in our simulations, we set this at a level typical of graduates from existing boot camp programs).

Not surprisingly, the most important factor affecting prison bed-space requirements is the probability that participants would be imprisoned if the boot camp did not exist. In boot camps that have typical in-program and postrelease failure rates, the probability of imprisonment for those admitted has to be around 80 percent just to reach a break-even point—that is, to have a net impact of zero on prison bed space. In other words, in order to begin to reduce prison bed-space requirements, more than 80 percent of those admitted to boot camps would have to serve prison terms if the boot camp did not exist. Substantial reductions in prison bed space require even higher probabilities of imprisonment.

As the probability of imprisonment drops, boot camps with typical failure rates substantially increase prison bed-space needs.

In New York, boot camps embody all the right design

options—the corrections department selects participants, big discounts are given, and large-scale boot camps are operated. Officials estimated in 1993 that New York's boot camps had reduced the prison population by about 1,500 inmates *below what it would have been without boot camps.* However, between 1988 and 1993 New York's total prison population rose by 16,000 inmates, an increase almost eleven times greater than the saving in bed space ostensibly due to boot camps.

As figure 1 in the appendix demonstrates, when in-program and postrelease failure rates are set at typical levels, a 200-bed, ninety-day boot camp in which entrants have a 10 percent probability of imprisonment will increase prison bed-space needs by 502.

These 502 new prison beds are needed to accommodate in-program and postrelease failures and to replace the 200 beds taken over by the boot camp. In most boot camps 30 to 40 percent of the entrants are removed for disciplinary violations or voluntarily withdraw. Typically, these in-program failures serve full regular prison terms. If their probability of imprisonment is very low to begin with, in-program failures quickly accumulate into a sizeable block of new inmates, most of whom would not have been in prison at all if the boot camp did not exist.

Because their populations turn over so rapidly, boot camps expose a large number of offenders to the risk of failing in the program and of serving a substantial prison term. A 200-bed, ninety-day boot camp can admit almost 900 inmates a year. If each in-program failure serves one year of imprisonment, those failures alone would raise total prison population by 273 inmates.

POLICY IMPLICATIONS

If officials intend to use boot camps to reduce prison bed-space needs, four policy implications are clear.

1. Eligibility and Selection. First, boot camps should recruit offenders who have a very high probability of imprisonment.

To do that, officials could change eligibility criteria, selection procedures, or both.

Eligibility criteria could target offenders convicted of violent crimes; property offenders with multiple prior felony convictions; probation violators who have multiple prior felony convictions; offenders who would get presumptive prison terms under statewide sentencing guidelines; or offenders who have served prior prison terms.

These criteria differ starkly from those commonly used today for prison boot camps. In many states, statutes limit boot camp eligibility to nonviolent first offenders. These criteria were lifted directly from older shock probation laws, which were based on an assumption that a short "taste" of prison will deter young impressionable offenders from future crime. That assumption is unsupported and in some cases has been refuted by empirical evidence.

Unfortunately, these deterrence-based selection criteria virtually assure that boot camps will increase, not diminish, the need for prison beds, because no state sends 80 percent of its nonviolent first-time felons to prison.

Selection procedures could be changed so departments of corrections pick boot camp participants from among incoming inmates who have been sentenced to regular prison terms. In most states, this also means the parole agency will be the releasing and supervising authority.

States should avoid letting judges select boot camp participants at sentencing. In states where judges pick boot camp participants, practitioners candidly admit that most boot camp participants would have gotten probation if the boot camp did not exist.

2. Failure Rates. The second policy implication is that boot camps should minimize failure rates, consistent with the needs to maintain program discipline and to instill pride among those inmates who complete the difficult regimen. This could be done by reducing in-program and post-release failures.

Boot camps might refuse to let inmates withdraw voluntarily during the first two or three weeks, when their muscles are most sore. They might institute a wide range of sanctions within the program, or set up segregation cells, so they can punish a broader range of rule violators within the boot camp. The object should be to expel only the most chronic violators.

Many states intensively supervise boot camp graduates. If the states respond reflexively and revoke all detected violators, intensive supervision enables officials to detect more violations (especially more minor violations). Supervision could be altered to emphasize support more than surveillance. States could structure revocation policies for boot camp graduates, so that they use an array of swift and certain sanctions that do not involve reimprisonment. Reimprisonment could be reserved only for serious or chronic violations.

3. Sentence Reductions. The third policy implication is that boot camps should select inmates who will receive a substantial reduction in time served for completing the boot camp.

Selecting more serious or persistent offenders for boot camps (the first implication) will also increase the "discount" offenders get from completing the boot camp. Officials also might use boot camp participation as a way offenders can shorten a minimum prison sentence that otherwise would be mandated by law. These reductions must be based on actual time served, not maximum potential imprisonment terms, and the reductions must be real, not illusory. Real and substantial reductions are easiest to measure in states that use objective guidelines or criteria to set release dates. For example, under New York's parole guidelines, boot camp graduates typically shave eighteen to twenty-four months off their minimum parole dates. If the reductions were small—say, only three or four months—few prison beds would be saved. In addition, inmates would have much less incentive to volunteer for the boot camp.

Politicians are likely to accept big reductions in prison terms for these types of inmates only if boot camps go to extraordinary lengths to address these inmates' higher levels of needs and problems. Hence, an important reason for emphasizing provision of treatment and services in boot camps is to build political support for shorter confinement terms.

4. Size. Assuming the first three implications are addressed, the fourth is that a large-scale boot camp operation is needed to make a substantial dent in a state's prison population.

A fifty-bed boot camp will have no discernible impact in a state with 12,000 prison inmates. At best, its impact will be overwhelmed or masked by scores of other factors that affect population. But even a large boot camp that embodies all these prescriptions cannot assure lower prison populations: other factors (such as major changes in sentencing laws or enforcement patterns for offenders not eligible for boot camps) may drive up the prison population and force a state to fund new construction anyway. Of course, if the first three implications are not heeded when states design boot camps, running small boot camps will at least minimize the growth in prison population that will result.

Boot camps designed to reduce crowding probably will cost considerably more to operate than regular prisons. Savings in operating costs require that the total person-days of confinement be reduced (e.g., graduates would be confined only four months rather than two years). There also may be savings by cost avoidance—eliminating the need to build new prisons.

SUMMARY

There is no evidence that boot camps significantly reduce recidivism rates. If officials want to use boot camps to cut crowding, boot camps need to be fundamentally redesigned:

- Officials should recruit offenders with a high probability of imprisonment.
- Correctional agencies that operate prisons should select participants; judges should not.

- Boot camps should recruit offenders who will get substantial reductions in prison terms for completing the boot camp.
- Boot camps should provide intensive treatment, programming, and services.
- In-program failure rates should be minimized and aftercare should emphasize long-term support.
- Boot camps that fit the above profile should be operated on a big scale.

If this configuration of boot camps is not politically viable, and if corrections officials are serious about reducing prison populations, they should oppose new or expanded prison boot camps. If they don't, boot camps almost certainly will increase prison populations, worsen crowding, and divert us from other policies that may work better.

The model and documentation are available free of charge from Dale G. Parent, Senior Analyst, Abt Associates, Inc., 55 Wheeler Street, Cambridge, MA 02138.

APPENDIX

Figures 1 and 2 project the prison bed savings or needs associated with boot camps of different sizes and durations under different assumptions.

Figure 1 shows projections of need for prison beds associated with operation of a 200-bed, ninety-day boot camp. The projections make assumptions, based on the average documented experience of existing boot camps, of what proportion of offenders who complete the programs will breach release conditions and be reincarcerated and of the average length of the period of reincarceration.

Figure 1 has two axes. One indicates the net change in prison beds, and the other shows the average probability of imprisonment facing boot camp inmates had the boot camp not been available.

The two curves in figure 1 show different projections based on 15 percent or 40 percent rates of failure within the program. The 40 percent assumption is more realistic in light of experience to date.

Figure 1: 200-Bed, Ninety-Day Boot Camp (9-month reduction)

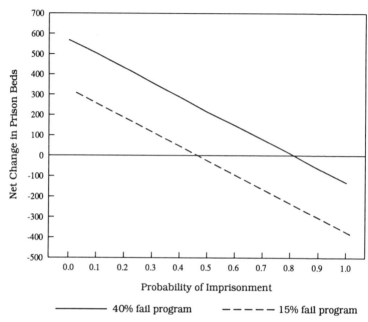

On the optimistic assumption of a 15 percent failure rate, most boot camps for first offenders would increase prison populations. Only if 45 percent of persons admitted were otherwise bound for prison would the jurisdiction break even on demand for beds. On the more realistic assumption of a 40-percent failure rate, the break-even point would be reached only if 80 percent of admittees were prison-bound.

Figure 2 shows similar projections for a 1,500-bed, 180-day program. The break-even points relative to prison admission probabilities occur at slightly lower levels, but overall, except for programs in which admissions are decided by prison officials from among confined offenders, the chances of increasing populations are greater than those of reducing populations.

Figure 2: 1,500-Bed, 180-Day Boot Camp (24-month reduction)

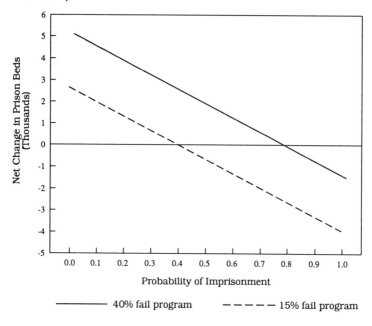

40% fail program ——— 15% fail program — — — —

Boot Camps—A National Assessment
Doris Layton MacKenzie

There are more than forty-seven state boot camp prisons, two in the Federal Bureau of Prisons, ten in local jails and prisons, and at least six for juvenile offenders. In 1988, eight state boot camps—in Florida, Georgia, Illinois, Louisiana, New York, Oklahoma, South Carolina, and Texas—agreed to participate in a study of their effectiveness. The study, which I conducted with support from the National Institute of Justice, was designed to identify the programs' goals and to investigate to what extent the goals were achieved. The study examined the implementation and program development, attitudinal changes of participants, recidivism and positive social adjustment during community supervision, and effects on prison crowding. This article summarizes the findings.

Boot camps have two primary goals—to change offenders and to reduce prison overcrowding. The principal findings are that most programs produce positive attitudinal changes in participants, have few if any effects on participants' subsequent criminality, and are likely to reduce prison crowding only if program admissions are tightly controlled to assure that spaces are allotted to prison-bound offenders.

Most programs targeted young offenders convicted of nonviolent crimes. Participation was limited to those who were mentally and physically able to participate in a rigorous daily schedule of activities. Programs differed substantially in whether and to what extent participants engaged in rehabilitative programs, in whether participation was voluntary, in the nature and quality of supervision after release, and in how offenders were selected for admission (e.g., by judges or departments of corrections).

ATTITUDE CHANGE DURING INCARCERATION

The attitudes of offenders were examined once at the beginning of their time in the boot camp prisons and again near the end. These changes were compared to attitudinal changes of offenders serving time in traditional prisons.

The results indicated that offenders in boot camp prisons leave the prisons less antisocial than they were before they entered. There was some evidence that program characteristics such as availability of rehabilitative opportunities, program rigor, and voluntariness can produce greater reductions in antisocial attitudes.

Boot camp graduates typically became more positive about their experiences and their future, and believed they had changed for the better. The results were surprisingly consistent. Graduates both from the programs emphasizing physical training and work and from programs incorporating significant rehabilitation, treatment, and education components felt positive about their experiences.

The attitudes of comparison groups of offenders serving time in traditional prisons also became less antisocial while in prison. However, unlike the boot camp offenders, prisoners' attitudes toward their experiences and the future did not become more positive. They typically did not report that their experiences in prison had been beneficial.

INFLUENCE ON RECIDIVISM

The recidivism rates of offenders who graduated from the boot camps were compared to the recidivism rates of others who were dismissed and to rates of similar offenders serving time on probation or parole. The findings are shown in figures 1a and 1b, which, for each state, shows revocations (generally separately for new crimes and technical violations) for boot camp graduates, for offenders who failed to complete the boot

Figure 1a: Recidivism Rates of Boot Camp Graduates and Comparison Groups in Oklahoma, Texas, Florida, and Georgia

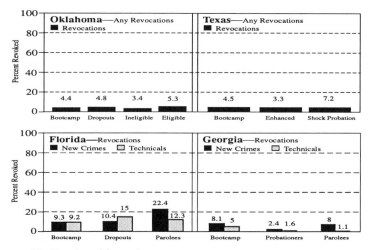

Source: MacKenzie and Souryal 1994.

Figure 1b: Recidivism Rates of Boot Camp Graduates and Comparison Groups in South Carolina, New York, Illinois, and Louisiana

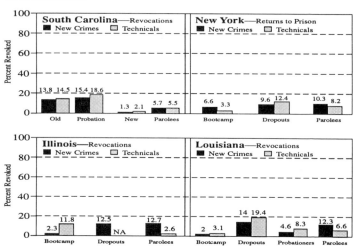

Source: MacKenzie and Souryal 1994.

camp programs, and for one or more comparison groups. In general, the recidivism rates of offenders who successfully completed the boot camps were similar to those of comparable offenders who spent a longer time in prison or who were given a sentence of probation. In programs in which boot camp offenders had lower recidivism rates, the differences could not be attributed to the effect of the military atmosphere.

Recidivism rates varied greatly depending on how long offenders were in the community, the method of measuring recidivism, the type of correctional sanctions, and the state being examined. Of the boot camp graduates, 23 to 63 percent were rearrested in the first year of supervision, 1.3 to 13.8 percent were revoked for new crimes, and between 2.1 and 14.5 percent were revoked for technical violations. Because of variations in the different states' programs and in the evaluations of each, no meaningful inferences can be drawn from comparisons of recidivism rates between states.

In five states there was no evidence that the boot camp experience had an effect on recidivism. As shown in figure 1a, Oklahoma and Texas boot camp releasees were no less likely to recidivate than comparison offenders (the differences were not statistically significant). Besides comparing the boot camp offenders with shock probationers, the Texas study compared the performances of offenders who received an "enhanced" boot camp program of substance abuse treatment with the performance of offenders in an earlier (preenhanced) boot camp. There were no differences. However, the increased time devoted to treatment in the enhanced programs was still very small (less than one hour per day for some inmates) in comparison with boot camps in other states (which often had three or more hours per day devoted to rehabilitation).

There were no differences between the Georgia boot camp releasees and parolees, but releasees were more likely to be revoked for a new crime than a sample of probationers. This was the only case when the boot camp releasees had higher recidivism rates than the comparison groups. The Georgia program emphasized the military atmosphere of the boot camp but included only minimal therapeutic activities. It stood out from the other programs in terms of the little time devoted to education, counseling, or drug treatment. (Since that time there have been major changes in the Georgia boot camps.)

Although the recidivism analyses for the Florida and South Carolina programs show lower recidivism rates for boot camp graduates than for the comparison groups, analyses suggested that there were systematic differences between the boot camp offenders and the comparison samples. The boot camp graduates may simply have been drawn from lower-risk groups of offenders. As a result, any differences could not be attributed to the program itself. In Florida, there were no differences in recidivism rates between the graduates of the program and the dropouts. They both did better than a comparison group of parolees. That the graduates and the dropouts had comparable experiences probably indicates that they were different from the parolees before they went into the program. It is unlikely that the boot camp could have influenced the dropouts, since most of them left during the first two weeks.

During the course of the study, South Carolina made a major change in the way participants were selected. Originally, the probation department designated participants. During the latter part of the study, the department of corrections designated boot camp participants from persons entering prison. The operation of the program remained the same.

Data were collected in South Carolina from probationers, parolees, boot camp releasees from the original program, and releasees after the program changed. The recidivism analyses indicated that when boot camp participants were selected from among probationers, their behavior during the community supervision was similar to that of probationers (see "Old" South Carolina comparison in figure 1b). However, when participants were selected from among prisoners, they performed identically to parolees from prison and not like the probationers (see "New" comparison). Differences between boot camp releasees and others probably resulted from preexisting differences in the characteristics of the participants and the comparison samples, not from the effects of the program.

The recidivism rates of the New York boot camp graduates did not differ from the parolee comparison sample in arrests or returns to prison as a result of a new crime. However, the boot camp graduates were less likely to be revoked for a technical violation. New York had developed an "After-Shock" program that provided intensive supervision along with enhanced aftercare opportunities for counseling, drug treatment, and employment. Possibly this was why technical violations fell.

Boot camp graduates from Illinois and Louisiana were less likely to be revoked for a new crime. In Illinois the boot camp graduates were more likely to be revoked for a technical violation than were members of the comparison samples. This was true of Louisiana also, except when the intensity of supervision was controlled in the analysis (see figure 1b). Thus, it appears that if the groups had been supervised at the same level of intensity they would have received the same rate of technical violations. This was not the case with the new crime revocations.

If a highly regimented atmosphere by itself (with strict rules and discipline, physical training, and hard labor) reduced the recidivism of offenders who completed boot camp, releasees should have lower rates of recidivism than comparable offenders receiving different sentences. This did not happen. Thus, we concluded that the boot camp atmosphere alone does not reduce recidivism, nor does it result in higher recidivism than characterizes those who spend a longer term in prison.

There were some commonalities among the three states (Louisiana, Illinois, New York) where the boot camp releasees had lower rates of recidivism on some measures. In these programs, all offenders received intensive supervision after they were released from the boot camps. None of the other programs we studied did this. These three programs had a strong focus on rehabilitation (three or more hours per day), high dropout rates, voluntary participation, selection from prison-bound entrants, and they were the longest programs. It was not possible to untangle the specific effects of these program components combined with the military atmosphere.

IMPACT ON POSITIVE ACTIVITIES

One of the hypothesized advantages of boot camps is that they will engender a heightened sense of personal responsibility and accountability. We examined the community adjustment of the boot camp releasees using an index measuring their success in pursuing employment, education, residential and financial stability, and treatment. The supervising probation or parole agents evaluated the offenders on these measures during the first year of supervision in the community. Their performance was compared to samples of parolees, probationers, and prisoners who were dismissed from the boot camps.

We had data from five states: Florida, Georgia, Louisiana, New York, and South Carolina. We found no differences between boot camp releasees and the comparison samples in four states. Only in Florida did the boot camp releasees adjust better during community supervision. Our examination of the Florida program did not reveal any significant differences from programs elsewhere that would lead to this effect.

During the first year of community supervision, the performances of both boot camp graduates and comparison samples declined over time. The more intensely these offenders were supervised in the community, the better their adjustment. This may indicate that parolees can be coerced by criminal-justice personnel to take part in positive activities during community supervision.

IMPACT ON PRISON CROWDING

Data from five states were used to estimate the savings or, conversely, the loss of bed space that resulted from the boot camp programs (MacKenzie and Piquero 1994). The model made use of recidivism rates, duration of imprisonment, dismissal rates, and program capacity to estimate the impact of the program. The probability that the offenders would have been in prison or on probation was varied to examine the effect.

Results indicated that boot camps can reduce prison crowding if they are designed so that entrants are selected primarily from offenders who would otherwise have been in prison. If program entrants were chosen from offenders who would have been on probation, the programs would not save beds but require additional ones. Figure 2 shows for New York, for example, the different effects on prison-bed savings or need that result from different assumptions about the extent to which participants are diverted from regular prison. If few of the participants would otherwise have been in prison, there is a loss of bed space. If all of the offenders would have been in prison, prison beds are saved.

Figure 2: Effects on Prison Bed Needs of Prison Diversion Rates, New York

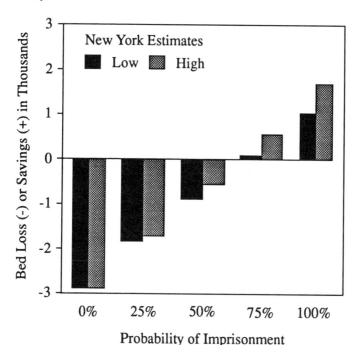

Source: MacKenzie and Piquero 1994.

We examined the effects of other changes in assumptions. One was to reduce recidivism rates by one half. There was no evidence that the boot camps would reduce prison crowding through such a reduction in recidivism. Even if recidivism rates were reduced by 50 percent, the model predicted little additional savings in prison beds. The major variance affecting crowding was whether the programs targeted offenders who were prison-bound.

We investigated the placement decisions within the five states. In three states—New York, Louisiana, and Florida—offenders entering boot camps were sentenced to prison, and department of corrections officials later selected participants for boot camps. The programs were used as an early release mechanism, allowing some inmates to earn their way out of prison earlier than their earliest possible release date.

The bed-space model estimated bed savings in two states: New York and Louisiana. There was little evidence that the Florida program would save prison beds. The number of beds saved by these programs was a result of the dismissal rates, program capacity, and decrease in time served for the offenders who successfully completed the boot camp. Florida's program failed to save prison beds because a large number of offenders were dismissed prior to completing the boot camp, and those who did complete the boot camp did not serve substantially less time than similar offenders who had spent time in traditional prisons. Essentially, any bed-space savings came through using the boot camp as an early release option.

In South Carolina and Georgia the court placed offenders in the boot camps. As noted earlier these results refer to the early boot camps in these states; since the time of data collection for this study the two programs have changed tremendously. We concluded that many of the offenders who entered the boot camps would have been given probation if the boot camps had not existed. Therefore, most likely these two programs increased the demand for prison beds. We estimated that the South Carolina program cost the prison system between 52 and 174 beds. The Georgia program required between 30 and 230 additional beds.

SUMMARY

We do not know yet how to organize boot camps with reasonable confidence that they will achieve their intended results. We do not know if they can be done right. The eight-state assessment does suggest how *not* to organize boot camps. The only effects on recidivism that were found were in programs that included a strong rehabilitative component in the daily schedule of activities (three or more hours) and programs that provided intensive supervision to participants after release.

Programs designed only to provide physical training, hard labor, and military discipline did not reduce recidivism; and, considering the results from the Georgia program, they may have a negative impact.

The structure and discipline of the boot camps in combination with the focus on rehabilitation and intensive aftercare may enhance the effect of treatment. Whether this is the case remains an open question. Reports from inmates on attitude measures and in interviews suggest that their experiences in these boot camps may be more positive (but much more stressful) than the experiences of those in traditional prisons.

Only carefully designed programs will reduce crowding. This reduction will come not from reducing recidivism but from reducing the time offenders spend in prison. Boot camps could be used to permit some offenders to earn their way out of prison earlier, thus saving prison beds for more serious, violent offenders.

Support for boot camps continues to grow. The eight-state assessment does not provide strong support for their continued growth without careful monitoring and evaluation to learn whether they are achieving their goals. The administrators who agreed to cooperate with this study and similar research currently in progress in New York, Illinois, Georgia, and the California Youth Authority deserve credit for being willing to ask the right questions. They will be in the forefront in developing successful correctional programs because they are willing to learn how to do it right.

NOTES

For more detailed information about the boot camps in this study and the selection of sites, see MacKenzie and Souryal (1994) and MacKenzie (1990). Data were collected between 1987 and 1990. There have been many subsequent changes in boot camps in these states. Additional information can be obtained from state departments of corrections or in the following reports: New York State Department of Correctional

Services 1992, 1993, 1994; Florida Department of Corrections 1989; Flowers et al. 1991; Illinois Bureau of Administration and Planning 1991; Louisiana Department of Public Safety and Corrections 1992; South Carolina State Reorganization Commission 1992.

The data analyses were done using parametric survival analyses measuring time to failure. Because the assessment did not use an experimental design, variables were entered in the model to control for differences among samples. There are major differences among programs and in data collection and analyses; comparing rates across sites presents serious problems of interpretation.

My collaborators and I are grateful to the correctional administrators and staff who participated in the evaluation. Researchers in each state were supportive at every stage. This investigation was supported in part by Grant #90-DD-CX-0061 from the National Institute of Justice, Office of Justice Programs, U.S. Department of Justice, to the University of Maryland. Points of view in this document are those of the author and do not necessarily represent the official position of the U.S. Department of Justice.

3

Home Leave in Northern Ireland

Vacations for "Terrorists"

Brian Gormally and Kieran McEvoy

Ten years ago Brendan "Bik" McFarlane was one of the most wanted men in Europe. He had been imprisoned for blowing up a bar in which five people were killed. He was commanding officer of the Provisional IRA prisoners during the hunger strikes in 1981. In 1983 he led a mass breakout of thirty-eight IRA prisoners from the Maze (Long Kesh) prison. Recaptured in the Netherlands, he was extradited back to Northern Ireland amid worldwide publicity to become the most notorious "high-risk" prisoner in the system. He remains a committed IRA volunteer who considers himself a prisoner of war with a duty to escape.

Yet this summer he was released for a week-long "holiday" with his family and friends. He returned peacefully on time to prison to resume his sentence and presumably to resume his efforts to escape.

So how is it that one of Europe's most notorious captured "terrorists" can be permitted a week-long vacation among Belfast's shops and perhaps a quiet drink in one of its many bars?

This is only one of the most dramatic examples of the operation of the Northern Ireland prison system's unique "home leave" scheme. Every summer and Christmas approximately one third of Northern Ireland's prison population are released unsupervised for a week. All prisoners are allowed periods of home leave in the last year of their sentence, in order to assist in preparing for release. They are helped to get jobs and can reexperience family life before final release. But it is the offering of summer and Christmas vacations to long-term prisoners, most of whom will serve many more years before release, that is the unusual feature. Prisoners who have served eleven years of a determinate or indeterminate sentence are eligible for this scheme.

Of course, the Northern Ireland prison population is an unusual one after twenty-five years of political violence. The IRA has continued its campaign of violence against what it regards as British occupation of the North of Ireland. Loyalist (Protestant) paramilitaries, who wish to maintain the link between Northern Ireland and Britain, continue their own campaign against Catholics whom they perceive as sympathetic to the IRA and its objectives. The result is a prison population that consists of at least two thirds political prisoners, many serving long sentences.

Those who maintain their allegiance to their respective paramilitary organizations consider themselves political prisoners. Such prisoners are held in segregated groups. They are organized in military structures. All negotiations with the authorities are done through their own commanding officers. The prisoners wear their own clothes, do no prison work, and exercise a considerable degree of autonomy as to how they spend their days.

These committed political prisoners are the main beneficiaries of the home leave scheme. So far not a single paramilitary prisoner has failed to return in the years of the scheme's operation.

It may seem curious that paramilitary prisoners, with their duty of escape while in prison, voluntarily walk out of their prison and walk back, twice a year. It is equally paradoxical that the authorities feel they can release "terrorists" for a summer or Christmas vacation but maintain that they are too dangerous to be released finally.

In practice, the authorities rely on the discipline of paramilitary prisoners. For they will neither escape nor become militarily reinvolved during the period of furlough and risk ruining the scheme for their comrades. Ordinary nonpolitical prisoners in Northern Ireland (colloquially known as ODCs—"ordinary decent criminals") are extended the same privileges and, predictably, small numbers of them periodically fail to appear on time. This does not, however, jeopardize the overall operation of the scheme.

The home leave scheme is only one of the more dramatic examples of a modus vivendi between politically motivated prisoners and the authorities in Northern Ireland.

The managers of the prison service have adopted a policy that we have termed "normalization." This accepts the existence of mutually hostile groupings of politically motivated prisoners in the system and takes on the task of managing them with the least possible confrontation.

The prisoners' paramilitary command structures accept the need to offer a level of cooperation to the authorities and to pursue political demands in ways that minimize suffering to themselves and their families.

The management of an abnormal situation in which the majority of prisoners are politically motivated, serving long sentences for serious offenses, is thus "normalized" in the sense that it becomes just one of numerous problems the service managers must deal with. Others, for example, include the overuse of short-term imprisonment to deal with fine defaulters, the management of significant numbers of sex offenders, and chronic labor relations problems with prison officers.

The central thrust of this approach to management is to avoid unnecessary conflict and to use the uniqueness of the paramilitary prisoners to facilitate their better management. It is not an explicit acceptance of the IRA's demand that its members be recognized as political prisoners. Neither is it a policy of appeasement based on ill-defined liberal principles. It is a pragmatic and hard-edged decision to swallow a few ideological misgivings for the sake of better-run prisons and the removal of the prisons from the front line of the Northern Ireland conflict.

This approach is in sharp contrast to the era between 1976 and 1981, when the authorities had a deliberate policy to delegitimize political prisoners. This meant the rigid enforcement of all the symbols and regimes of ordinary prisoners, such as the wearing of prison uniforms and the doing of prison work. IRA prisoners refused and thus began the spiral of deteriorating relations that led to hunger strikes in 1980 and 1981. Bobby Sands and nine other men starved themselves to death to protest these symbols of criminality. Eighteen prison officers were murdered by the IRA, and there were forty-eight related violent deaths in the community.

This period was a political disaster for the British authorities. They experienced worldwide condemnation for their perceived intransigence, and the IRA cause gained its highest level of popularity during the current conflict. As a result, during the next two years, the prison authorities quietly granted virtually all of the prisoners' demands. These concessions formed the basis of a new style of management. The negative consequences of repression and counterviolence, based on a struggle over symbols and ideology, led to an appreciation of the benefits of pragmatism and de facto cooperation.

It would be wrong to give the impression that conflict and violence have disappeared from Northern Ireland's prisons. Outbursts of deadly violence occur between prisoner factions and between them and prison officers. This is perhaps inevitable, given the nature of the prison population. Some would argue that the authorities have, at times, failed to learn the lessons of their own successes.

However, Bik McFarlane had his week of liberty this summer. As in other political conflicts around the world, the fate of politically motivated prisoners will be key to any solution of the problems of Northern Ireland. What the home leave scheme and other aspects of normalization within the prisons demonstrate is that, with political will and policies directed by pragmatism rather than rigid ideology, deals can be struck between apparently irreconcilable enemies. Perhaps Northern Ireland's prisoners and prison managers have lessons to offer those further removed from political violence and its consequences, who yet have the political responsibility for a resolution of the conflict as a whole.

5

CLIENT-SPECIFIC PLANNING

Introduction

If probation agencies were adequately funded, there would be no need for client-specific planning, commonly referred to as CSP. Probation agencies in many jurisdictions, however, are demoralized and have suffered drastic reductions in resources in recent decades. Federal judges and court orders and law-and-order politics focus the attention of public officials on prisons and jails, and—whether they like it or not—they must find new sources of funds to house steadily growing numbers of inmates. Powerful policy arguments can be made for increased investment in probation agencies and in any number of treatment programs, but these inevitably are less persuasive than federal court orders. Probation agencies have difficulty resisting cuts in their budgets to pay for increased spending on institutions and are seldom successful in arguing for substantial increases.

The results of decades of inadequate funding in many jurisdictions include average caseloads of 150 to 300 probationers per officer, increased reliance on fees collected from offenders, inability to invest in promising new programs, and high rates of officer burnout. Were it not for these problems, CSP would have little role to play.

Client-specific planners serve as a link between judges and

community-based sanctioning resources. Generally they work for the defendant and his lawyer, though occasionally they work directly for the judge or for a prosecutor. Their mission is to shape a sentence that wins the judge's support because it simultaneously acknowledges the seriousness of the offender's crimes, addresses offender characteristics that contributed to his troubles (drug abuse, alcohol), provides restitution and solace to the victim, and increases the offender's chances of living a productive, law-abiding life. In developing proposed sentencing plans, planners typically interview the offender and his family, the victim, and the offender's current and former employers and teachers, and canvass local resources that can be employed in administering the sentence. Often these include private and public medical, counseling, educational, and welfare services that are not connected to the criminal-justice system. Often the proposed plan also includes informal supervision by a family member or an employer. Often the planner does the legwork and files the applications to assure that, if the plan is approved, the treatment slots, supervisors, and community service jobs are available so that the proposed sentence can be carried out.

Many people become probation officers because they want to work with and help people, and many would like to devise presentence investigation reports (PSIs) and sentence recommendations as rich, detailed, and imaginative as those prepared by the best planners. In practice, however, many probation officers do well to prepare perfunctory PSIs based on victim and offender interviews and FBI rap sheets. A probation officer cannot do in a few hours what the planner does in a week or more. As a result, few probation officers can make the time to track down a treatment program uniquely matched to the offender's needs or to find scarce treatment or training slots, reserve them for the defendant, and figure out how to pay for them.

Although many judges and prosecutors are suspicious of planners, because they are seen as partisan employees of the defendant, planners have been remarkably successful in having their plans adopted by judges. This is because the plans cannot be put into effect unless the judge so orders, and the planners must therefore devise plans that judges will find credible and that do not expose judges to charges of undue leniency. The articles by Marc Mauer describe an innovative yet typical sentencing plan for a defendant charged with attempted murder and give some idea of the explosive spread of client-specific planning in recent years.

Not surprisingly, planners are in great demand by affluent and white-collar defendants who are willing to pay whatever it costs to avoid a prison sentence. However, many people drawn to CSP as a profession come from social service and criminal-defense backgrounds and want services such as theirs to be made available to disadvantaged offenders. Foundation funding, especially from the Edna McConnell Clark Foundation, has supported pilot and training projects in a number of states. Support for CSP programs has been won in some states (e.g., Missouri) and in some counties (e.g., many in North Carolina) by persuading public officials that CSPs can achieve net cost-savings by diverting offenders from prisons and jails to community-based sanctions. In some jurisdictions, public defenders have added planners to their staffs on the rationale that effective representation should extend beyond the adjudication phase to sentencing.

CSP poses a dilemma for probation officials, and that dilemma has been a serious impediment to the spread of CSP. Many probation officials see CSP as a competitor and argue vigorously that planners do nothing that probation officers cannot do and that public resources for sentence planning should go to the probation agency and not to an independent or outside agency. The difficulty is that probation is so seriously underfunded that additional funds for CSP are likely to face pressing bureaucratic competition from champions of other worthy and unmet probation needs (for example, getting caseloads down to a point where meaningful supervision is possible). As a consequence, it is difficult for probation agencies to deliver planning services as effective as those that can be provided by special-purpose outside agencies and by independent professional planners hired on a case-by-case basis. Despite these problems, CSP has spread rapidly in both the United States and Canada. The article by Matthew Yeager offers an overview of the findings of evaluations of CSP programs and discusses the problems CSP has had in attracting continuing financial support from government.

Defense-Based Sentencing

Marc Mauer

The glamour of criminal defense or prosecution lies in the unusual case that goes to trial. For the more than 90 percent of convictions that result from plea bargains, however, the sentence that will be imposed is the most critical element of a case for a defendant. Yet criminal lawyers seldom receive training in sentencing.

With tremendous problems of prison and jail overcrowding now facing almost every state, sentencing has become more critical than ever. Programs and policies designed to address this need have been developed in many jurisdictions. One of the more successful approaches has been called defense-based sentencing. It is an approach to sentencing that combines the skills of the defense attorney with the creativity of a new breed of sentencing professionals, in an attempt to offer sentencing judges a greater range of options than had traditionally been available.

Defense-based sentencing began more than twenty years ago in some locations. Its most immediate impetus, though, dates from the introduction of the client-specific planning (CSP) approach to sentencing that was pioneered by the National Center on Institutions and Alternatives in 1979.

The basic premise of CSP is that each defendant coming

before a judge for sentencing is a unique individual. He or she has a particular family background, social history, and set of circumstances that led to the commission of the crime. These considerations are no excuse for criminal activity, but they can serve as a starting point for tailoring a sentence to the individual.

Working with a defense attorney, a sentencing specialist develops an individualized sentencing plan that speaks directly to the needs of the victim, the offender, and the community. Sentencing plans vary according to the case, but generally involve some or all of the following elements: short-term or intermittent incarceration or work release, supervision, fines, restitution, community service, treatment conditions (drug, alcohol, mental health, or other counseling programs), residential conditions, employment and education conditions, or other restrictive conditions (house arrest, forfeiting the right to drive or consume alcohol, restrictions on contact with certain people or places).

The sentencing plan is then presented to the judge as an option for sentencing that is more restrictive than probation. The judge is free to accept the proposal in whole or part, or to reject it and sentence the offender to prison.

Defense-based sentencing programs using variations of the CSP approach have spread rapidly. In 1980, there were fewer than 20 defense-based sentencing programs in the country. Today, there are more than 115. A survey conducted by The Sentencing Project in Washington, D.C., found that these programs now handle over 16,000 felony cases a year, with 8,000 receiving intensive case-planning services.

The most important indicator of success for these programs is acceptance by sentencing judges. Of more than 6,000 cases handled by the National Center on Institutions and Alternatives since its inception, over two thirds have resulted in sentencing plans that were accepted by the courts. Similar success rates have been achieved by most other programs.

Studies of several state programs have demonstrated that

defense-based programs are having a substantial impact on the number of offenders being sentenced to prison. Researchers at the Institute of Government of the University of North Carolina at Chapel Hill have examined that state's defense-based sentencing programs. They concluded that almost 70 percent of defendants served by twelve locally based programs were likely to have received a prison term if not for the services of the program. About half of all defendants received a sentence involving no prison time, and another quarter received prison terms of six months or less. Overall, 90 percent of the sentencing plans proposed by the programs were accepted in full or in part by sentencing judges.

Judges throughout the country praise alternative sentencing programs for providing them with new options between prison and probation. Superior Court Judge Coy E. Brewer, Jr., of Fayetteville, North Carolina, has said:

> . . . the greatest concern I have had in sentencing is the paucity of sentencing options that I would face in a particular situation. These programs create a continuum of punishment options with more gradations in them, so we have the possibility of meaningful community-based punishment. (Mauer 1990)

"Love Made Me Go There, Whiskey Caused Me to Shoot Her"—The Alabama Seventeenth Judicial Circuit Sentencing Project

Marc Mauer

The Seventeenth Judicial Circuit, centered in Linden, Alabama, lies an hour west of Selma. Judge Claud Neilson is the only circuit court judge for the three-county jurisdiction. Largely rural and poor, the area has only limited resources. Yet, owing to the interest of Judge Neilson and others in the local criminal-justice system, it is the site of an innovative sentencing program.

The pilot project, begun in the fall of 1989, was funded by

the Edna McConnell Clark Foundation to determine whether sentencing options could be developed for persons who would otherwise go to prison in a rural area, and whether local community support could be generated.

The main premise is that for many defendants, individualized sentencing proposals can be developed that better meet the needs of justice than does incarceration. Grady Wacaster, a former prison warden and now director of a sentencing program in North Carolina, has been working with defense attorneys and others in the seventeenth Judicial Circuit to develop sentencing options in a number of difficult cases. One of his first cases illustrates the program's potential.

Willie Collins is a fifty-seven-year-old black resident of Faunsdale, where he has lived all his life. He and his common-law wife of more than thirty years have eleven children. Recently, they separated. After Collins learned that his wife intended to marry another man, he went to visit her at her home. Already inebriated, Collins got into an argument with her, pulled out a gun, and shot her. After wounding her, Collins shot himself in the stomach. He was arrested and charged with attempted murder. Asked by a reporter why he had committed the crime, Collins replied, "Love made me go there, whiskey caused me to shoot her."

After being contacted by Collins's attorney, Wacaster spent many hours getting to know Collins. He also spoke with Collins's employer and others in the community who knew him, and looked into the situation of the victim and her children. Wacaster found that Collins lived in a one-room house with no electricity, for which he paid $15 a month rent. Although Collins could neither read nor write, he had been employed at local dairies for more than twenty years, often working seven days a week. Collins appeared to be an alcoholic, but this did not interfere either with his getting to work on time or with his performing his work satisfactorily.

While recognizing that Collins had committed a serious

offense, Wacaster believed that a sentence that did not involve imprisonment could respond better to the needs of the victim, the offender, and the community.

For the victim, Collins's former wife, restitution of $100 a month for five years was to be taken from his pay at the dairy. Collins would be forbidden contact with her.

For the community, Collins would perform 100 hours of unpaid community service at the local fire department, supervised by the mayor of Faunsdale.

For Collins himself, the sentencing proposal recommended a number of controls to ensure public safety. Recognizing Collins's alcohol problem, the sentencing recommendation didn't propose what might have seemed an obvious solution—an alcohol treatment program. Instead, Wacaster recommended that Collins not be permitted to drink anywhere except in his own home. At his age, Collins was probably not going to stop drinking. He could, however, be persuaded to control his drinking, and, along with a ban on possessing firearms, be prevented from committing a similar offense. He would be subject to a breathalyzer or drug test when requested.

Collins was also required to maintain his employment, pay fines and fees to the court, and be placed under probation supervision for five years.

The proposal was presented in court, with testimony from a number of witnesses. One of these, a dairy operator, described why he believed that incarceration was not necessary to punish Collins: "Ain't nothing no worse than dairy. They hadn't got anything over there [in prison] that bad."

After hearing arguments from the district attorney and defense, Judge Neilson concurred with the recommendations and imposed a sentence incorporating the elements of the sentencing proposal.

The sentencing of Collins did not have a significant impact on Alabama's prison overcrowding, nor did it attract major headlines outside the area. What it did accomplish was to demonstrate the potential for creative sentencing.

Client-Specific Planning in Delaware
Timothy Roche

Cornelius Harley is a thirty-seven-year-old homeless black male with a history of severe alcoholism and a lengthy juvenile and adult criminal record typified by theft and punctuated with occasional violence. He has been incarcerated several times and has failed repeatedly on traditional probation.

This general profile may sound familiar, because it is. There are thousands of Cornelius Harleys locked up in state prisons across the country. What sets this case apart from countless others like it was its disposition.

On October 5, 1990, Cornelius Harley was again facing sentencing, this time for assaulting another homeless man with a boxcutter as they argued over who would sleep in a vacant building. But something special happened in the courtroom of Wilmington Superior Court Judge Richard Gebelein: rather than impose a lengthy prison term, Judge Gebelein sentenced Harley to a structured set of community-based sanctions designed to hold Harley accountable for his behavior while addressing its root cause—his alcoholism.

The alternative sentence imposed on Harley grew out of recommendations provided to the court by the new Wilmington office of the National Center on Institutions and Alternatives (NCIA). With funding from the Edna McConnell Clark Foundation, NCIA has begun to prepare client-specific plans for three inmate populations: (1) defendants at sentencing whose offense and background are such that they would otherwise be prison bound, (2) pretrial detainees who otherwise would be likely to remain incarcerated, and (3) prison inmates who are eligible for parole but otherwise are unlikely to be released.

In Harley's case, NCIA recommended a suspended prison

term and a six-month halfway house commitment, during the first three months of which Harley would participate full-time in an intensive outpatient alcohol treatment program. During the second three months Harley would be allowed to engage in part-time employment with a local contractor, while continuing in alcohol treatment twenty hours per week. Later, as Harley's release from the halfway house approached, arrangements would be made to have Harley receive the assistance of Neighborhood House, a local agency that helps needy individuals secure stable housing. Intensive probation supervision was also recommended to begin upon release from the halfway house, supplemented by monitoring by Black Man's Development, Inc. Eighty hours of community service with Habitat for Humanity was also proposed. Finally, a former employer of Harley's will act as a mentor and provide one-on-one supervision and assistance during the difficult time ahead.

Harley's was the first case completed by the new client-specific planning project in Delaware. Over eighteen months, NCIA will present similar proposals on 240 cases in the three inmate groups.

Optimism is high. Client-specific planning has proven effective in jurisdictions across the country. Delaware officials who have been exposed to its potential see no reason why it can't also work for them.

Perhaps the unique quality of NCIA's individualized approach is the human perspective it offers. On the surface, for instance, Harley might have seemed a poor candidate for an alternative. But detailed background information revealed areas of strength upon which to build. Harley's alcoholism began at age thirteen and was exacerbated by a physically abusive home environment. Forced to quit school and begin working at an early age, Harley became a skilled carpenter who was, when sober, said to be a good worker. Former employers spoke well of him, always noting, however, his debilitating alcoholism.

In designing the proposed alternative, NCIA staff pursued

Harley's fragments of community support and exploited his skills. From what appeared to be a nearly "hopeless" case, NCIA helped build a credible plan, one that Harley is both thankful for and committed to. "I've never been offered a chance like this before," he told Judge Gebelein at the sentencing hearing. "There's no way I'll fail the program or myself."

The project's long-term success, like Harley's, won't be known for some time; but in both cases, the potential for meaningful and lasting change is within reach.

Client-Specific Planning in the U.S. and Canada
Matthew Yeager

Client-specific planning (CSP) programs successfully achieve most of their objectives, according to a recent review of twenty-seven evaluations of CSP programs released by the Solicitor General's Office of Canada. CSP is a form of intensive sentencing advocacy designed to develop detailed, intermediate-sanction proposals for jail-bound defendants.

The survey's most significant findings were that judges accept proposed sentencing plans in upwards of 70 percent of cases, that offenders subject to sentencing plans have no worse recidivism rates than do comparable confined offenders, and that CSP offers promise as a device for reducing North America's overreliance on imprisonment. Despite their success, however, CSP programs have had difficulty achieving long-term stability and funding. CSP programs are often resisted and undermined by traditional criminal-justice institutions, including the courts and probation officers. In at least twelve of the twenty-seven studies surveyed, there was evidence of destabilization of CSP programs by prosecutors, probation departments, departments of correction, legislators, and bar associations. Some of the CSP programs were simply shut down; others have had to struggle to survive. Overt hostility—usually of a "turf" nature—was often recorded, with probation departments being the most vocal in their opposition.

ACCEPTANCE OF PLANS

No doubt much of the opposition comes from concern that CSP programs will compete with existing programs for funds and from recognition that CSP's success in developing credible sentencing plans somehow calls the effectiveness of other agencies into question.

CSP has been successful in gaining support from judges. In the sixteen studies that report such statistics, a mean of 70 percent of proposed sentencing plans were accepted in full or in part by the courts. The CSP experience shows that judges want more information and are prepared to use it.

DIVERSION

CSP programs appear to have diverted prison-bound offenders to community sanctions. However, little of the available research is sufficiently rigorous to support stronger conclusions. Only seven of the twenty-seven studies used a control group for comparison purposes. Four of those studies showed that members of the CSP groups were less likely to be sentenced to confinement. Two other studies reported no difference in diversion but concluded that CSP defendants received shorter jail sentences than did defendants in a control group.

RECIDIVISM

Only eight of the twenty-seven studies reported any recidivism data; only in one did the CSP sample do worse on recidivism than a control sample. For the most part, no significant differences in recidivism emerged.

COSTS

Data from North Carolina suggest that the average cost of a CSP plan in that state was approximately $2,189. That is well under the $12,000–$30,000 annual per-capita cost of imprisonment in North America. Standing alone, CSP programs increase the per-client costs of public defender or legal aid systems. However, the proper cost-effectiveness comparison is with per-capita correctional budgets. In an efficient system of cost accounting, a portion of the corrections budget that would be spent on an offender's imprisonment should be credited to CSP each time a CSP client is diverted from prison.

NET-WIDENING

Some CSP programs have merely "widened the net" because clients have not been restricted to prison-bound offenders. Others have succeeded in overcoming this problem by restricting intake to serious offenders who demonstrate a high probability of being imprisoned. Staff in North Carolina CSP projects use an empirically derived classification instrument to calculate the probability that a client will be imprisoned. Intake can then be restricted to the most serious, prison-bound cases.

IMPLEMENTATION ISSUES

During the start-up of a CSP project, attention should be focused on training and resource identification. It is important that community resources be inventoried to identify "placements" prior to accepting cases.

It might be useful to offer CSP training to probation department staff so that they could better understand the technique. This might foster less resistance to its implementation.

The use of personnel from other agencies, including the probation department, might help ameliorate tensions, enhance credibility, and increase productivity.

Judges expect some follow-up data on CSP cases in order to justify their continued use of the technique. This means that CSP units must establish "tracking" systems to follow the status of each case and periodically update that information. Tracking is also effective in identifying those offenders who need "patchwork" done to their CSP plans. It is not uncommon, especially in juvenile work, for changes to be needed to a CSP plan.

Most CSP case developers should probably be full-time staff. One or more supervising case developers should be hired to maintain quality control and generally to oversee casework. Referral sources, such as the defense bar, should be educated on the benefits of early referral and on the use of a mitigation hearing at sentencing, with the case developer available in court.

IMPLICATIONS

Client-specific planning is but one technique for managing criminal offenders. It is neither a panacea nor a cure-all, and by itself probably does not reduce recidivism rates. CSP has the potential to educate the public about the benefits of a reparative model of punishment.

The debate between proponents of retributive versus reparative justice may well continue to escalate during this decade—especially given the overwhelming costs of incarceration. CSP has had a positive impact as a general method of sentencing advocacy for prison-bound offenders. But there is little hope for lowering incarceration rates without a reallocation of existing resources to intermediate sanctions.

Copies of Matthew G. Yeager's report, "Survey of Client Specific Planning," are available from Research and Program Development, Corrections Branch, Solicitor General of Canada, 340 Laurier Avenue West, Ottawa, Ontario, Canada KIA OP8; (613) 992-8421.

6

COMMUNITY
CORRECTIONS
ACTS

Introduction

Community corrections acts are a product of the fragmentation of governmental authority and financial responsibility concerning the corrections system. Throughout most of this century, the fragmentation has not much mattered. From 1920 to 1970, prison and jail populations fluctuated within narrow bands. State governments typically had responsibility for prisons and parole and county governments had responsibility for jails and probation. County governments had to pay to administer jail sentences and the state had to pay for prison sentences. This created potential tensions, which occasionally flared when judges were pressured by local officials to send more offenders to state prisons in order to reduce pressure on county facilities and finances. Conversely, crowded state facilities sometimes resulted in backups in county jails of offenders sentenced to prison, thereby effectively shifting the costs of their confinement from the state to the county. Overall, however, through the 1960s these were relatively low-level if endemic problems.

The rough equilibrium shattered, beginning in the 1970s, for reasons that are discussed below. First, however, it may be useful to offer a somewhat fuller sketch of the divisions of function and responsibility that characterize state criminal-justice systems. Compared with most countries, such as England and Wales, which have a single nationally funded judicial system and a single nationally funded corrections system, American states follow no common pattern.

In every state, the judiciary is organized hierarchically, with the same rules and procedures applying in every courtroom, with one set of applicable laws, and with a system of appellate review to settle disagreements; but there is no standard organization of corrections. The state always runs and pays for the prison and parole systems. Typically the state prisons hold convicted offenders serving terms of one year or longer, and the county jails hold pretrial detainees and convicted offenders serving terms under one year. There are, however, exceptions; Pennsylvania, where convicted offenders can be sentenced to up to five years in the county jail, is the extreme case. In most states, county governments operate and pay for county jails, but here too there are exceptions. In a minority of states, including Delaware and Alaska, all institutional corrections programs are the responsibility of a state department of corrections. Such systems are referred to as unified corrections systems.

The diversity becomes greater when noninstitutional programs such as probation, parole, and various intermediate sanctions are taken into account. Parole, supervised release after completion of a prison sentence, is the easy part; in the more than forty states where it exists, parole is a state responsibility. There are in addition a few states, including Pennsylvania, in which counties operate parole programs for jail inmates.

The organization of probation is more complicated. In a few, not all, of the states having unified corrections systems, the state department of corrections also operates the probation system; Delaware is an example. In some states, a state department of probation operates all probation programs. In other states, probation is the responsibility of county governments; management responsibility may be lodged in the county sheriff's department, in an independent probation agency, or occasionally in the local judiciary. In still other states, including Minnesota, probation in some counties is managed by the state and in other counties by county agencies.

Generalizations about intermediate sanctions are even harder to offer. Intensive supervision programs, for example, have been operated by courts, by local probation departments, by state probation departments, by state departments of corrections, and by state departments of parole. House arrest, electronic monitoring, and community service likewise are found in many different agencies at both state and local levels.

This fragmentation of management and financial responsibility often impedes efforts to establish or implement corrections policies. For example, federal court orders may limit the number of prisoners who may be confined in a state facility, and population analyses may show that many current prisoners could safely and less expensively be handled in local programs. The rational solution, and the most cost-effective, would be for states to encourage counties to establish local programs for otherwise prison-bound offenders and to transfer state funds to the counties to pay for them. The net burden on the state's taxpayers would be less than if those offenders were handled by the state.

The rational solution, however, seldom happens. From the perspective of a tax-sensitive state governor or legislator, locally funded programs are free; conversely, from the perspective of a tax-sensitive county executive or council member, state-funded programs are free. Since most public officials prefer that other public officials accept responsibility for increasing taxes to pay for needed new programs, the result often is that state officials try to divert offenders to the counties without providing funds to pay for them, and local judges send offenders to state programs to protect local resources.

Three developments have converted these chronic frictions

into fundamental, immobilizing conflicts that community corrections acts—efforts to shift state funds to counties in order to implement state policies—are designed to address. First, beginning in the 1960s, federal courts abandoned the hands-off doctrine that protected state prisons from judicial scrutiny. The resulting prisoners' rights movement resulted in hundreds of decisions declaring practices in state prisons unconstitutional, establishing minimum management standards, and establishing prison population caps. Since 1980, at any one time prisons in thirty-five to forty states have been subject to federal court orders. This has meant that problems of prison (and jail) conditions and overcrowding cannot be ignored.

Second, beginning in the late 1970s, many states began to develop sentencing guidelines. Initially, developers concentrated on the questions of which felony offenders should be sent to state prisons and for how long, and on the implementation of standards of statewide application that would minimize disparities in sentencing. More recently, guidelines developers have begun work on misdemeanor sentencing (which means county jail) and on intermediate sanctions. These developments have meant that the problems of noncoordination and financial conflicts of interest between state and local officials can no longer be ignored; otherwise comprehensive statewide systems of sentencing guidelines will be unachievable.

Third, and most important, law-and-order politics of the past twenty years has led to calls for imposition of harsher sentences by judges and to passage of harsher sentencing laws by legislators. As a result, the number of people in prisons and jails more than tripled between 1980 and 1994. Federal courts have limited the extent to which officials can confine more people without accepting political responsibility for increasing taxes to pay for constitutionally adequate facilities.

These three developments have made the traditional patterns of noncooperation and efforts to shift funding responsibility between states and counties inherently unstable and ultimately unsustainable. Community corrections acts are an effort to provide a system for developing statewide policies that are in the state's political and governmental interest while providing a mechanism for encouraging counties to develop local programs to carry out state policies and for shifting state funds to the counties to pay for them.

The first community corrections act was enacted in Minnesota in 1973, and by 1994 more than twenty states had followed Minnesota's lead. The concept has received more rhetorical than financial support from state governments, and progress has been slow. State officials often express frustration at what they see as local foot-dragging and grudging cooperation. Local officials often complain about what they see as unreasonable state policies and insufficient state funding.

Some states are doing much better than others, and many states that do not have community corrections acts are considering their adoption. In some states (Oregon, Kansas, and Minnesota are examples), community corrections acts are well established. Supporters claim that they have led to creation and expansion of important programs, have successfully diverted offenders from state prisons, and have saved public funds. Whether these claims can be substantiated is unclear; the evaluation literature is slight and unsophisticated.

In the articles that follow, Mary Shilton gives an overview of the development of community corrections acts and summarizes findings from the major evaluations; Dennis Schrantz describes the early stages of implementation of a community corrections act system in Michigan; and Paul Friday and Michael Brown describe the political problems that corrections officials often encounter in trying to establish new community corrections programs.

Community Corrections Acts
Mary K. Shilton

Since Minnesota adopted the first community corrections act (CCA) in 1973, at least seventeen other states have passed legislation. The list now includes Alabama, Arizona, Colorado, Connecticut, Florida, Indiana, Iowa, Kansas, Michigan, Minnesota, Montana, New Mexico, Ohio, Oregon, Pennsylvania, Tennessee, Texas, and Virginia. The American Bar Association has approved a model community corrections act to encourage other states to pass laws largely based on the Michigan statute.

Proponents of correctional reform have long debated the merits of counties taking on the task of retaining and punishing sentenced offenders who would otherwise go to state prisons. Communities demand stricter penalties because they are concerned about punishing and deterring crime. Yet state prisons are inappropriate and too costly for many nondangerous offenders, and it is clear that prisons are criminogenic. Some progress in balancing these competing factors has been made by states and counties operating under community corrections acts.

Community corrections acts create a network of decentralized correctional programs for specific types of offenders. They are mechanisms by which state funds are granted to local governments and community agencies to foster local sanctions to be used in lieu of state incarceration.

States with community corrections legislation have the advantage of an allocation and administrative structure to encourage program development. Legislation can also provide incentives to overcome county suspicions and interagency competition for scarce funding.

Existing state community corrections laws differ in their purposes and emphasis. Oregon's emphasizes a rehabilitative philosophy and an effort toward decentralized programs. Florida's recently passed law is geared toward introducing sanctions within a centralized system. Some acts stress probation reforms such as intensive supervision, and others stress intermediate sanctions or alternatives. Michigan targets both nonviolent felons and misdemeanants who are jail- or prison-bound. A major goal of the Michigan program is to relieve jail crowding in order to retain at the local level more nonviolent felons who historically get pushed into the state system to relieve jail pressures.

Each successful implementation of a community corrections act requires both adequate resources and concerted state and local efforts. During the early 1970s, steadily increasing prison and jail populations and the withdrawal of federal funds from the Law Enforcement Assistance Administration prompted several states to restructure state and local probation, parole, and correctional services. In 1966, the California Probation Subsidy program, in which state funds were paid to the localities for prison-bound inmates kept in local programs, was designed to reduce commitments to state prison by increasing county probation services. The program subsidy was in effect until 1978, when it was repealed because the reimbursement failed to keep pace with growing county costs for probation. During the past two years, California has once again been studying community corrections subsidies through a Blue Ribbon Commission and statewide focus groups.

The Minnesota Community Corrections Act illustrates what can be accomplished when adequate subsidy levels and state/local cooperation underwrite a sustained effort. The Minnesota act provides participating counties with substantial funding for probation and decentralized correctional services. The trend has been for participating counties to pay for a greater proportion of community corrections programs. In 1979 the state provided 37 percent of total funding under the act. In 1990 it provided 22.6 percent. Despite this trend of increased county financing, participating counties continue to support the program because it is more cost-effective than prison. Probation supervision in community corrections act counties costs between $1 and $100 per day, and state prison costs between $48 and $138 per day. Evaluations of similar programs in Oregon, Kansas, Virginia, Iowa, and Indiana have shown reductions in admission rates to prison of offenders targeted for community corrections programs.

The difficulties of diverting otherwise prison-bound felons should not be underestimated. Increasingly, CCA states are attempting to design sophisticated data collection systems that will measure impact. For this to be workable, however, data showing a "snapshot" of the criminal-justice system must be obtained first. This has been called a "policy-driven, data-informed decision-making process."

Although many community corrections acts were designed in part to deal with prison crowding and costs, these laws alone cannot do that job. Two community corrections act states have adopted felony sentencing guidelines as an additional reform to reduce prison crowding. In Minnesota and Oregon, analysis of community corrections populations prompted a reexamination of sentencing practices and development of felony sentencing guidelines to help relieve prison crowding.

Participating communities, through community corrections advisory boards, develop a forum for local input on correctional treatment programs. These boards bring responsibility for correctional decisions to the county level and underscore the relevance of correctional decisions. Community corrections acts not only make economic sense in hard times, they improve a fragmented justice system by providing information about programs that work and where improvements are needed. Programs aimed at public safety and prevention of high-risk behavior can be part of the effort. Community corrections, coupled with sentencing reform, offer the best hope for a correctional system facing unprecedented challenges. The burden is on state and local decision-makers to recognize this opportunity and to support community corrections.

Michigan's Community Corrections Act
Dennis S. Schrantz

The Michigan Community Corrections Act (CCA) of 1988 established a statewide policy for funding locally developed and operated corrections programs to divert nonviolent offenders from local jails and state prisons. The law created the Office of Community Corrections (OCC) to work with local units of governments that will oversee local community corrections advisory boards, administer grants, and monitor programs funded under the act. OCC began full operations in January 1990. Community corrections advisory boards now cover seventy-nine of Michigan's eighty-three counties.

The OCC, local governments, and local community corrections advisory boards are working to educate their publics about the benefits of diverting nonviolent offenders from incarceration and to make them aware that community corrections programs cost less to operate than jails and prisons and do not threaten public safety.

The overall goals of the OCC are to reduce the number of admissions to jails and prisons of nonviolent offenders where appropriate; to use local jail resources more cost-effectively; and to gain widespread support of the Community Corrections Act and community corrections programs from leaders in government, criminal justice, and the private sector. The CCA assumes a link between jail and prison crowding; when jails become crowded, counties increase the number of felons sent to the state. The counties that send the most short-term, nonviolent felons to the state are all experiencing severe jail crowding. In Wayne County, which sends the most short-term felons, jail has not been a local sentencing option for nearly five years.

Jail and prison crowding are facets of "system crowding." Courts, probation officers, public defenders' offices, prosecutors, policy agencies—all facets of the criminal-justice system—are crowded with more offenders than they can handle. To look at a crowding problem outside of the context of system crowding is shortsighted.

During the current fiscal year OCC will commit more than $10 million to local "comprehensive corrections plans." Of Michigan's 83 counties, 79 participate in the act under 52 community corrections advisory boards. Of these, 44 have developed and approved comprehensive plans.

OCC's aim is to divert people from prison safely and appropriately. During the first full year of implementation of the comprehensive plans, we expect to divert about 400 persons from state prisons. Next year we hope to divert 1,300 people.

Programs are funded in three general categories: community-based programs, jail-based programs, and offender services. Services differ from programs in that the money from OCC purchases services—for example, drug treatment to an offender in a residential probation program—rather than pays for agency operational costs.

Criminal-justice reforms have failed time and again because of inattention to "widening the net." This happens when persons who would otherwise have been put into probation are placed in "alternatives." When the alternatives are applied to the otherwise probation-bound offender, and that offender fails—which is often the case, since he is under closer scrutiny—the offender may then be put into prison. When this happens, the goals of alternatives are turned on their heads. This is a sad fact of many alternatives: they have increased prison admissions rather than decreased them.

To avoid net-widening, programs must do a better job at targeting—that is, making certain that only persons who otherwise would be sent to jail or prison are placed in the diversionary programs. Targeting must include collection of data that clearly separate the target population from all others.

More important than the type of program is the population it targets. The act targets only prison- or jail-bound offenders who would have been incarcerated in a state or local correctional facility had the community corrections option not been available. Examples include offenders convicted of a nonassaultive property offense; drug offenders and other nonviolent offenders where addiction is indicated; probationers or parolees detained for technical violations; adult felons and misdemeanants; program or parole violators and juvenile offenders sentenced as adults who do not pose a physical risk to public safety; and offenders who have not demonstrated a pattern of violent offenses or behavior.

Since the act's primary purpose is diversion of institution-bound offenders, perhaps the single most important question to ask in any community is, What is the definition of the jail- or prison-bound offender? Since the criminal-justice system varies from community to community, this definition varies widely. The policies of the State Community Corrections Board and OCC guidelines, however, specify a process for local communities for establishing community-specific definitions of jail- and prison-bound offenders before they decide how to respond to jail and prison crowding.

The act requires evaluation of its effects. Evaluation is difficult because of difficulty in answering the question, Who are the jail- or prison-bound offenders? The only defensible position is that this definition will differ for each community, since social mores, community histories, and local responses to crime vary widely. The definitions of "jail-bound" and "prison-bound" necessarily are dictated by community conventions and values.

A common process is being followed across the state in establishing community-specific eligibility. First, local data are collected and analyzed that establish the characteristics of the people in jail and prison (the target population compared to other offender groups). These characteristics then become eligibility criteria for community corrections programs.

Major issues that evaluations of diversion programs must address are the extent to which the programs have succeeded in keeping target-category offenders out of jails and prisons or have kept prison admissions low; the extent to which the programs have been successfully implemented in terms of established goals and objectives; and the extent to which communities differ in achieving success with diversion programs, and the reasons for these differences.

Part 6   Community Corrections Acts

Traditionally, Michigan had no capability for monitoring use of local jails or community corrections programs or to determine the effects of diversionary programs. To satisfy the statutory requirement to demonstrate impact of the programs, OCC designed and implemented new and sophisticated data systems. OCC, assisted by grants from the National Institute of Corrections, has designed and recently begun to implement both a Jail Population Information System (JPIS) and a Community Corrections Information System (CCIS).

Local decision-making in Michigan regarding use of jails and admissions to prison will never be the same. During the period when OCC worked to educate local judges, prosecutors, probation representatives, defense attorneys, and others, prison admissions for short-term felons dropped slightly. This, I think, is a positive indication that something is happening.

Assessment of Community Corrections Acts
Mary K. Shilton

Since Minnesota passed its community corrections act (CCA) in 1973, a growing number of states (at least twenty by 1994) have recognized the need to provide funding and statewide support for innovative community programs to punish offenders. Community corrections acts are mechanisms that provide state subsidies and coordinate the development of intermediate sanctions and diversion programs. In most states they transfer monies to localities and private agencies to operate programs for offenders who might otherwise be in prison or jail.

Recent audits and evaluations have examined CCAs in Colorado, Kansas, Michigan, and Texas. The findings affirm the value of such legislation. However, two emerging forces in community corrections have yet to be fully reviewed by statewide audits: the value of county-based management and support, and the role of private nonprofits in innovation (Shilton 1993). Most audits focus instead on four major issues: goals, funding, accountability, and implementation. These factors seldom consider other system problems addressed by CCAs.

UNREALISTIC EXPECTATIONS

Community corrections acts do not restructure correctional agencies, probation, or parole. They do not change criminal procedure, sentence terms, or authority to punish. Nonetheless, community corrections acts are expected to put an entire correctional system in order.

Setting goals to guide the development of community corrections is critical to its success. CCA goals relate to every other step in the process, from assignment of roles to agencies to evaluation of outcomes. Successful CCAs are characterized by shared approaches and negotiated strategies to implement objectives.

If expectations are unrealistic, failure is certain. In a 1992 review of the Michigan Community Corrections Act, the auditors concluded that the goals of the act were unrealistic in expecting drastic reductions in prison populations without establishment of sentencing guidelines tied to prison capacity; such systems take years to refine (Huskey et al. 1992).

DEVELOPING GOALS

Although state CCAs are remarkably similar in their enumerated goals, priorities are often unclear, and experts admit to confusion. Statewide community corrections acts typically list the following goals: preserving public safety, reducing the numbers of offenders sent to prisons or jails, punishing effectively, increasing sentencing options, reducing costs, improving local/state programs, and enhancing planning, coordination, and management.

In theory, such objectives are translated into program priorities by cognizant state agencies, state advisory boards, and local coordinating councils.

The more decentralized the program, the more likely it is that goals will vary within a state. Part of this is due to differences among jurisdictions within a given state, and part to the transfer of authority to local jurisdictions to create a range of community-based correctional services.

When typical state CCA goals are put to the scrutiny of an evaluation, they seldom receive high marks for clarity or precision. Often they are vague, inconsistent, general, and confusing. For example, a review of the Kansas Community Corrections Act noted the "boilerplate" goals statement in contrast with the perception of Kansas leaders that the real goal was to reduce commitments of nonviolent offenders to state prisons (Harris, Jones, and Funke 1990). This contradiction has since been observed in interviews of administrators in nearly every other CCA state.

But the hodgepodge of goals is not without some compensating benefit. It allows states and counties wide latitude in planning and funding intermediate sanctions that fit their perceived needs. However, it also reduces the likelihood that uniform, statewide measures will be achieved or sought. Broadly stated goals may aggravate interjurisdictional or interagency rivalries for funding, because everyone competes for resources.

A Colorado auditor's report criticized ineffective multiple goals (O'Brien 1993). It concluded that Colorado's fragmented system was subject to "competing values of communities, victims, offenders, and individual agencies" that complicated operations. A survey revealed that public safety was the highest priority, followed by rehabilitation and restitution, but that these priorities were not always translated into funded programs. The report recommended that shared approaches be adopted to address common responsibilities and improve coordination.

STRUCTURAL REFORMS

One of the most difficult challenges for community corrections acts is to bridge traditional obstacles through shared powers. CCAs provide forums for interjurisdictional and structural problem-solving. Community corrections advisory boards and statewide coordinating councils do most of this work. In some jurisdictions, community corrections advisory boards have been so successful at improving programs that their county boards allocate additional funding.

Many of the problems cited in evaluations are contextual: they depend on the politics of the state, its sentencing laws, its interagency structure, and the responsiveness of its communities. CCA programs examine how various agencies view their functions vis-à-vis other agencies and begin to refine their roles.

For example, Colorado surveyed how similar problems were viewed by various agencies responsible for community-based systems. A number of specific perceived needs for collaboration were to improve delays in referral to programs, to develop a statewide records and monitoring system, to identify shared information and resource needs, and to complete a plan for centralized transportation management.

Similarly, the Michigan Corrections Act assessment in 1992 recommended that the state board adopt official policies, procedures, rules, and program regulations to facilitate recommended statewide steps to target prison-bound offenders and to develop an evaluation plan for statewide reduction of prison commitments and more appropriate use of jails.

The report of the Texas Punishment Standards Commission (1993) took a different course by recommending statutory "core services" to be required in participating jurisdictions.

FUNDING

Funding allocations are difficult for all CCAs. State audits reveal that funding should be realistic and the allocation mechanism simple—advice that is easy to offer and difficult to honor. Linking funding to outcomes has led to formulas, chargebacks, performance measures, and problems with verification of data. However, by contrast, entitlements and per diems have been criticized for failing to provide rewards for cost efficiency, targeting, and improved program performance.

Community corrections acts are subsidy programs, and most provide funding through counties. In some states, private nonprofit agencies receive direct funding, and in others the state operates its own programs. Funding levels must be sufficient to encourage participation unless the program is mandatory.

Funding of the Minnesota CCA is unique. Although the state has continued to invest in the CCA, the counties have been willing to pay a larger share over the years because of their involvement and control over spending (Minnesota Association of Counties 1992).

The 1993 Texas audit concluded that a dramatic increase in funding was needed. It also urged that the funding allocation mechanism be streamlined and not tied to the prison use formula that created an "entitlement."

The Kansas funding formula was roundly criticized both for being unrelated to program goals and performance and for being an inadequate basis for resource allocation. The use of chargebacks was seen by many counties as a penalty for judicial sentencing practices over which they had no control.

ACCOUNTABILITY

Effectiveness and accountability tend to be elusive issues for community corrections acts. Where there is a high level of decentralization and privatization, program standards must be negotiated and then monitored. The Colorado performance audit included a list of recommendations, including uniform data collection procedures, improved supervision of probationers, expedited fee collections, in-house disciplinary hearings, more uniform documentation of procedures, and timely reporting.

In Texas, the audit examined community corrections issues in the context of other sentencing concerns. It emphasized the need for sentencing reform coupled with more specific goals, objectives, and strategies, information objectives, a strategic plan, and a budget. This included measures of outcome and output.

In Kansas, the evaluation relied on a detailed statistical analysis and concluded that prison-bound populations were lowered due to the CCA and that there were some cost savings due to efficiencies and lower per-diem costs for community corrections.

In Michigan, the assessment concluded that overall effectiveness of the CCA depended on how the goals of prison and jail diversion were viewed. Among the CCA's accomplishments were its enlisting of full county participation in the program and a broad information effort to educate the public and officials about correctional problems in Michigan. It recommended streamlining the county application process and continuing to work on prison diversion.

Statewide audits offer an opportunity to view development of a community corrections act from the perspective of a team of outside experts. Some audits probe the consistency of goals and methods employed within a state. Others use a more analytical and scientific basis for evaluation. More recent ones measure the perceptions of those involved in implementation as well as those of criminal-justice or elected officials. They also offer suggestions for improved public and media relations. Although the Kansas report details improvements by counties, most do not fully explore the importance of collaboration between local governments and private agencies. The Michigan audit recognizes the value of a county-oriented approach. The concept of partnership must be reconciled with needs for efficiency and uniformity and should be a central concern of future CCA audits. Effective assessments will not be useful until they fully address underlying public safety and risk management issues that figure most prominently in the debate over how to punish offenders.

Part 6 Community Corrections Acts

The Politics of Community Corrections

Paul C. Friday and Michael Brown

The success of community corrections rests on how well programs are designed and implemented. The greatest risk is that community corrections funds will be used for new programming while courts and prosecutors continue to follow the same sentencing practices as before. To guard against this, community corrections managers must keep decision-makers, government officials, criminal-justice personnel, and community leaders informed of what is happening with the programs and why they warrant support and use.

The political rhetoric of the past decade has made the implementation of community-based sanctions extremely difficult. The public fears crime and frequently considers all offenders to be equally serious and dangerous. The "effectiveness" of the criminal-justice system is often measured in terms of whether jail and prison sentences are imposed, while increases in crime and recidivism are attributed to judicial and correctional "leniency."

Substantial investments have been made in community corrections in recent years, and a great deal has been learned about efficient and effective management and service delivery. The greatest challenges, however, are not managerial but political. Unless the general public supports community programs, few officials will feel comfortable doing so. Those who attempt to implement community corrections programs should keep the following political lessons drawn from experiences in several states in mind.

Work to overcome the justice system's isolation from the public. A corollary of isolation is ignorance. Although the public has generally been supportive of law enforcement, there is a broad distrust of other parts of the system. Little attempt has been made to link sanctioning in the public mind to any social values except punishment, and little effort has been made to clarify program goals and objectives.

The importance of realistic goals cannot be stressed too strongly. As a general rule, both the public and elected officials look for simple solutions to complex problems. Specific objectives are seldom set or announced for new programs, creating problems later in determining if they have worked.

Goals need to be related to specific problems identified through analysis of data on offender characteristics and needs, program components, and the program's recidivism "track record." Criminal-justice practitioners have the knowledge to set realistic goals, and therefore need to assist in bridging the gap between public knowledge and expectations for the system.

Don't underestimate neighborhood politics. Citizen groups have become increasingly active and place the needs of a small geographical area over the needs of the community at large. This NIMBY ("not in my backyard") phenomenon can frustrate creative and innovative programs on the basis of facility or program location alone.

While citizens may accept that community corrections is important in reducing jail and prison overcrowding, potential program sites that state or local justice leaders feel are appropriate are often not acceptable to local residents. The result is often a stalemate, with politicians feeling they must pander to voters' fears (often aggravated by "get tough" political campaigns) rather than support criminal-justice needs. Efforts to implement community corrections are no-win situations; some people don't like the idea of community corrections, and those who do don't want them in their neighborhood. These attitudes appear to be widespread.

This stance is understandable. Community corrections programs are often viewed by the public as increasing their probabilities of victimization, increasing crime rates and reducing property values. These concerns are particular problems when determining sites for residential facilities and halfway houses.

Showing people that research has repeatedly indicated that

crime rates do not increase nor property values decrease in neighborhoods having residential facilities may reduce opposition. Creation of "community advisory boards" may reduce resistance to residential facilities if the members are confident they know what is going on and feel they have a degree of control over what takes place in their own neighborhoods.

The prognosis for successfully implementing community corrections may not be as dubious as it appears. The chances of successful implementation increase significantly when concerns of the community are addressed.

A cooperative and trusting relationship needs to be achieved between community corrections personnel and judicial, prosecution, and law enforcement officials. Judges have enormous power. Community corrections is not, and should not be, involved in subverting or supplanting judicial discretion. But the effectiveness of alternatives is undermined if they are not used effectively—and they won't be unless community programs are respected by justice-system officials and are accountable to them.

The nature of crime and criminals has changed, and key criminal-justice players are elected, making it increasingly important to base community corrections programs on data rather than on testimonials. A data-based information system that incorporates both the characteristics of the offender population and an assessment of program outcomes provides the best "ammunition" to appeal to officials.

A better understanding of the nature of crime and offenders is needed. Research findings must work their way into decision-making so that empirical evidence forms a cornerstone of policy. Academics need to do more policy-oriented research that practitioners can trust. Both practitioners and academics have an obligation to educate the general public, who alone can rein in the political rhetoric. Education must address two subjects: knowledge of crime and offenders and knowledge of appropriate and effective responses.

Judges believe that offenders deserve jail time, but how

much time is effective or necessary to achieve justice? Despite the general failure of incarceration to reduce recidivism, there appears at least to be some comfort in being tough. Justice, therefore, becomes equated in many peoples' minds with punishment rather than with restitution or behavioral change. Recidivism and the fear of crime are what count, and for community corrections programs to thrive, their impact on recidivism must be demonstrated empirically.

Citizens must be helped to understand that crime is a local problem requiring local solutions. In most instances, offenders come from the communities in which they commit their crimes. They are, in important senses, products of the local community and responsibilities of that community. If they are sent to jail or prison, they usually return. Offenders are depicted as being significantly different from the rest of the population. Statistical representation of the local offender population can be used to generate a better understanding of crime as a local problem.

To this end the local media are an essential ally. Public education is critical, and one method of assuring the accuracy of the information generated is to spend time briefing those responsible for the dissemination of information. The public has been inundated with media stereotypes of offenders and offenses committed elsewhere. A local public education campaign based on empirical data and known research is necessary not only for community corrections to be accepted but also for it to be effective.

Every program must have adequate information and monitoring capacity. By statistically monitoring events, programs and policies can be changed and developed to meet local needs. Only by monitoring can operators know whether program slots are being filled by the kinds of offenders they were intended for and that something other than net-widening is going on.

Too many people fear data. But it is an ally and a resource. It protects what works and serves as a basis for discarding what does not work. Too few resources are available and too many of them are being wasted on ineffective programs that do not serve target populations because the population has never been clearly defined. And effective programs are under-used because they have never been evaluated. It is time to change this.

Bibliography

American Friends Service Committee. 1971. *Struggle for Justice: A Report on Crime and Punishment in America.* New York: Hill & Wang.

American Law Institute. 1962. *Model Penal Code,* Proposed Official Draft. Philadelphia: Author.

Baird, S. Christopher, and Dennis Wagner. 1990. "Measuring Diversion: The Florida Community Control Program." *Crime and Delinquency* 36: 112–25.

Ball, Richard A., C. Ronald Huff, and J. Robert Lilly. 1988. *House Arrest and Correctional Policy—Doing Time at Home.* Beverly Hills, Calif.: Sage Publications.

Barr, William. 1992. *The Case for More Incarceration.* Washington, D.C.: U.S. Department of Justice, Office of Legal Policy.

Baumer, Terry, Michael G. Maxfield, and Robert I. Mendelsohn. 1993. "A Comparative Analysis of Three Electronically Monitored Home Detention Programs." *Justice Quarterly* 10:121–42.

Baumer, Terry L., and Robert Mendelsohn. 1990. *The Electronic Monitoring of Nonviolent Convicted Felons: An Experiment in Home Detention, Final Report.* Report submitted to the National Institute of Justice, U.S. Department of Justice.

Beck, Allen, Darrell Gilliard, Lawrence Greenfeld, Caroline Harlow, Thomas Hester, Louis Jankowski, Tracy Snell, James Stephens, and Danielle Morton. 1993. *Survey of State Prison Inmates 1991.* Washington, D.C.: U.S. Government Printing Office.

Bureau of Justice Statistics. 1994. *Prisoners in 1993.* Washington, D.C.: Author.

Center for Applied Social Research of Northeastern University and Crime and Justice Foundation. 1988. *Evaluation of the Hampden County Day Reporting Center.* Boston: Crime and Justice Foundation.

Committee on Justice and the Solicitor General, Canadian House of Commons. 1993. *Crime Prevention in Canada: Toward a National Strategy.* Ottawa: Canada Communication Group.

Bibliography

Curtin, Elizabeth. 1990. "Day Reporting Centers." In *Intermediate Punishment: Community-based Sanctions*. College Park, Md.: American Correctional Association.

Curtin, Elizabeth L., and Jack McDevitt. 1990. *Massachusetts Day Reporting Centers Task Force: Final Report*. Boston: Massachusetts Executive Office of Human Services.

Davies, Malcolm. 1992. "A Policy Role for Focus Groups: Community Corrections." Sacramento, Calif.: Bureau of Criminal Statistics and Special Services.

Erwin, Billie S. 1987. *Final Evaluation Report: Intensive Probation Supervision in Georgia*. Atlanta: Georgia Department of Corrections.

Federal Bureau of Investigation. 1994. *Uniform Crime Reports for the United States—1993*. Washington, D.C.: Author.

Florida Department of Corrections, Bureau of Planning, Research, and Statistics. 1989. *Research Report: Boot Camp Evaluation*. Tallahassee: Author.

Flowers, Gerald T., T. S. Carr, and R. B. Ruback. 1991. *Special Alternative Incarceration Evaluation*. Atlanta: Georgia Department of Corrections.

Frankel, Marvin E. 1972. *Criminal Sentences: Law Without Order*. New York: Hill & Wang.

Galaway, B., and J. Hudson, eds. 1990. *Criminal Justice, Restitution, and Reconciliation*. Monsey, N.Y.: Criminal Justice Press.

Gormally, Brian, Kieran McEvoy, and David Wall. 1993. "Criminal Justice in a Divided Society: Northern Ireland Prisons." In *Crime and Justice: A Review of Research*, vol. 17, edited by Michael Tonry. Chicago: University of Chicago Press.

Harris, M. Kay, Peter Jones, and Gail Funke. 1990. *The Kansas Community Corrections Act: An Assessment of a Public Policy Initiative*. New York: Edna McConnell Clark Foundation.

Hillsman, Sally T. 1990. "Fines and Day Fines." In *Crime and Justice: A Review of Research*, vol. 12, edited by Michael Tonry and Norval Morris. Chicago: University of Chicago Press.

Home Office. 1990. *Crime, Justice, and Protecting the Public*. London: Author.

Hudson, J., and S. Chesney. 1978. "Research on Restitution: A Review and Assessment." In *Offender Restitution in Theory and*

Action, edited by B. Galaway and J. Hudson. Lexington, Mass.: D.C. Heath.

Hudson, J., and B. Galaway. 1989. "Financial Restitution: Towards an Evaluable Program Model." *Canadian Journal of Criminology* 31: 1–18.

Huskey, Bobbie L. 1984. "Community Corrections Acts Help Promote Community-Based Learning." *Corrections Today*, February.

Huskey, Bobbie, Kermit Humphries, and Mary Mande. 1992. *An Assessment of the Michigan Community Corrections Act*. Laurel, Md.: American Correctional Association.

Illinois Bureau of Administration and Planning. 1992. *Impact Incarceration Program: 1992 Annual Report to the Governor and the General Assembly*. Springfield: Illinois Department of Corrections.

Jones, Robert J., and Steven P. Karr. 1993. *Impact Incarceration Program: 1993 Annual Report to the Governor and the General Assembly*. Springfield: Illinois Department of Corrections.

Larivee, John J. 1990. "Day Reporting Centers: Making Their Way from the U.K. to the U.S." *Corrections Today*, October.

Lauen, Roger. 1990. "Community Managed Corrections." Laurel, Md.: American Correctional Association.

Lilly, J. Robert, Richard A. Bell, G. David Curry, and John McMullen. 1993. "Electronic Monitoring of the Drunk Driver: A Seven-year Study of the Home Confinement Alternative." *Crime & Delinquency* 39: 462–84.

Lilly, J. Robert, and Paul Knepper. 1993. "The Corrections-Commercial Complex." *Crime & Delinquency* 39: 150–66.

Lloyd, C. 1991. *National Standards for Community Service Orders: The First Two Years of Operation*. London: Home Office.

Louisiana Department of Public Safety and Corrections. 1992. *IMPACT: A Program of the Louisiana Department of Public Safety and Corrections*. Baton Rouge: Author.

McDonald, Douglas. 1986. *Punishment Without Walls: Community Service Sentences in New York City*. New Brunswick, N.J.: Rutgers University Press.

McIvor, G. 1992. *Sentenced to Serve: The Operation and Impact of Community Service by Offenders*. Aldershot, England: Avebury.

MacKenzie, Doris. 1994. "Shock Incarceration as an Alternative for

Bibliography

Drug Offenders." In *Drugs and Crime: Evaluating Public Policy Initiatives*, edited by D. L. MacKenzie and C. D. Uchida. Thousand Oaks, Calif.: Sage Publications.

MacKenzie, Doris. 1993. *Boot Camp Prisons in 1993*. National Institute of Justice Research in Action Release. Washington, D.C.: National Institute of Justice.

MacKenzie, Doris. 1990. "Boot Camp Prisons: Components, Evaluations, and Empirical Issues." *Federal Probation* 54: 44–52.

MacKenzie, D. L., and A. Piquero. 1994. "The Impact of Shock Incarceration Programs on Prison Crowding." *Crime and Delinquency* 40: 222–49.

MacKenzie, D. L., and C. Souryal. 1994. *Multi-Site Evaluation of Shock Incarceration: Executive Summary*. Report to the National Institute of Justice. Washington, D.C.: National Institute of Justice.

Maguire, Kathleen, Ann L. Pastore, and Timothy J. Flanagan, eds. 1993. *Sourcebook of Criminal Justice Statistics 1992*. Washington, D.C.: U.S. Department of Justice, Bureau of Justice Statistics.

Mair, George. 1988. *Probation Day Centres*. Home Office Research Study 100. London: H. M. Stationery Office.

Mair, George, and Claire Nee. 1992. "Day Centre Reconviction Rates." *British Journal of Criminology* 32: 329–39.

Mair, George, and Claire Nee. 1990. *Electronic Monitoring: The Trials and Their Results*. London: H. M. Stationery Office.

Mauer, Marc. 1990. "Defense-based Sentencing: Part of the Solution to Prison Overcrowding." *Overcrowded Times* 1(2): 8.

Maxfield, Michael, and Terry Baumer. 1990. "Home Detention with Electronic Monitoring: Comparing Pretrial and Postconviction Programs." *Crime and Delinquency* 36: 521–36.

Meachum, Larry R. 1986. "House Arrest: Oklahoma Experience." *Corrections Today* 48(4): 102ff.

Minnesota Association of Counties. 1992. "Why Minnesota Should Invest in Community Corrections." St. Paul, Minn.: Author.

Morris, Norval. 1974. *The Future of Imprisonment*. Chicago: University of Chicago Press.

Morris, Norval, and Michael Tonry. 1990. *Between Prison and Probation: Intermediate Punishments in a Rational Sentencing System*. New York: Oxford University Press.

Bibliography

Moxon, David, Mike Sutton, and Carol Hedderman. 1990. *Unit Fines: Experiments in Four Courts*. London: Home Office.

National Swedish Council for Crime Prevention. 1986. *Bulletin No. 3*. Stockholm: Author.

New York State Department of Correctional Services and the New York Division of Parole. 1994. "The Sixth Annual Shock Legislative Report." Unpublished report by the Division of Program Planning, Research, and Evaluation and the Office of Policy Analysis and Information. Albany, N.Y.

New York State Department of Correctional Services and the New York Division of Parole. 1993. "The Fifth Annual Shock Legislative Report." Unpublished report by the Division of Program Planning, Research, and Evaluation and the Office of Policy Analysis and Information. Albany, N.Y.

O'Brien, Timothy. 1993. *Community-Based Corrections System Performance Audit*. State of Colorado.

Parent, Dale G. 1993. "Boot Camps Failing to Achieve Goals." *Overcrowded Times* 4(4): 1, 12–15.

Parent, Dale G. 1991. "Day-reporting centers: An Emerging Intermediate Sanction." *Overcrowded Times* 2(1): 6, 8.

Parent, Dale G. 1989. *Day Reporting Centers—A Descriptive Analysis of Existing Programs*. Washington, D.C.: National Institute of Justice.

Pearce, Sandy, and John Madler. 1992. "A Compendium of Community Corrections Legislation in the United States." Laurel, Md.: American Correctional Association.

Pearson, Frank S. 1988. "Evaluation of New Jersey's Intensive Supervision Program." *Crime and Delinquency* 34: 437–48.

Pease, Ken. 1985. "Community Service Orders." In *Crime and Justice: An Annual Review of Research*, vol. 6, edited by Michael Tonry and Norval Morris. Chicago: University of Chicago Press.

Petersilia, Joan, and Susan Turner. 1993. "Intensive Probation and Parole." In *Crime and Justice: A Review of Research*, vol. 17, edited by Michael Tonry. Chicago: University of Chicago Press.

Reiss, Albert J., Jr., and Jeffrey Roth. 1993. *Understanding and Controlling Violence*. Report of the National Academy of Sciences Panel on the Understanding and Control of Violence. Washington, D.C.: National Academy Press.

Renzema, M. 1992. "Home Confinement Programs: Development,

Bibliography

Implementation, and Impact." In *Smart Sentencing: The Emergence of Intermediate Sanctions*, edited by J. M. Byrne, A. J. Lurigio, and J. Petersilia. Newbury Park, Calif.: Sage Publications.

Robinson, J. 1990. "Bill C-89: An Act to Amend the Criminal Code." Paper presented at the VIIth International Course on Victims and the Criminal Justice System, Dubrovnik, Yugoslavia.

Scottish Office. 1992. *Statistical Bulletin: Community Service by Offenders in 1990*. Edinburgh: Government Statistical Service.

Sechrest, Lee B., Susan O. White, and Elizabeth D. Brown, eds. 1979. *The Rehabilitation of Criminal Offenders: Problems and Prospects*. Washington, D.C.: National Academy Press.

Shilton, Mary. 1993. "Community Corrections Acts: Linking the Public and Private Sectors in New Partnerships." In *Community Partnerships in Action*, edited by Patrick McCabe. Laurel, Md.: American Correctional Association.

Shilton, Mary. 1992. "Community Corrections Acts for State and Local Partnerships." Laurel, Md.: American Correctional Association.

State Reorganization Commission. 1992. An Evaluation of the Implementation of the South Carolina Department of Corrections' Shock Incarceration Program. Columbia, S.C.: Author.

Texas Department of Corrections, Texas Adult Probation Commission, and Texas Criminal Justice Policy Council. 1989. "Special Alternative Incarceration Program: Enhanced Substance Abuse Component." Austin: Author.

Texas Punishment Standards Commission. 1993. *Final Report: Recommendations to the 73rd Legislature*. Austin: Author.

Thornburgh, Richard. 1991. "Introduction." In *Attorney General's 1991 Crime Summit—Summary*. Washington, D.C.: U.S. Department of Justice.

Tonry, Michael. 1993. "Sentencing Commissions and Their Guidelines." In *Crime and Justice: A Review of Research*, vol. 17, edited by Michael Tonry. Chicago: University of Chicago Press.

Umbreit, Mark S., and Robert Coates. 1993. "Cross-Site Analysis of Victim Offender Mediation in Four States." *Crime & Delinquency* 39: 565–85.

U.S. General Accounting Office. 1993. *Prison Boot Camps: Short-Term Prison Costs Reduced, But Long-Term Impact Uncertain.* Washington, D.C.: Author.

United States Sentencing Commission. 1994. *Sentencing Guidelines Manual.* St. Paul, Minn.: West Publishing.

van den Haag, Ernst. 1975. *Punishing Criminals: Concerning a Very Old and Painful Question.* New York: Basic Books.

Vass, Antony A. 1990. *Alternatives to Prison.* Newbury Park, Calif.: Sage Publications.

von Hirsch, Andrew. 1976. *Doing Justice: The Choice of Punishments.* New York: Hill & Wang.

Weigend, Thomas. 1993. "In Germany, Fines Often Imposed in Lieu of Prosecution." *Overcrowded Times* 4(1): 1, 15–16.

Weigend, Thomas. 1992. "Germany Reduces Use of Prison Sentences." *Overcrowded Times* 3(2): 1, 11–13.

Weitekamp, E. G. M. 1990. *Restitution: A New Paradigm of Criminal Justice or a New Way to Widen the System of Social Control?* Ann Arbor, Mich.: University Microfilms.

Wilson, James Q. 1975. *Thinking About Crime.* New York: Basic Books.

Winterfield, Laura A., and Sally T. Hillsman. 1991. *The Effects of Instituting Means-Based Fines in a Criminal Court: The Staten Island Day-Fine Experiment.* New York: Vera Institute of Justice.

Yeager, Matthew G. 1992. "Survey of Client Specific Planning." Ottawa, Ontario: Corrections Branch, Solicitor General of Canada.

Index

Index

allocations in, 195–96; goals of, 185, 192, 193–94, 199; politics of, 198–202

Community Corrections Information System (CCIS), 192

community service orders (CSOs), xii, 5–6, 48, 69–84, 132, 138; completion rates of, 76, 77–78, 80–81; costs of, 31; definition of, 72; evaluations of, 77–78, 80–84; as fines for indigents, 71; as incarceration diversion, 82–83, 174; as part of intensive supervision programs, 85, 89, 101, 128, 176; and recidivism, 76–78, 83, 84

Connecticut: community corrections acts in, 186; day fines in, 21, 26, 28–29; day-reporting centers in, 125–28

Connecticut Prison Association, 123

conservatives, 3, 4, 11

Corrections Services Incorporated, 115

costs: of community corrections acts, 189; of community service programs, 71, 83–84; cutting of incarceration, as goal of intermediate sanctions, 6, 8, 9–10, 13, 89, 94, 95, 103, 113, 122, 184; of incarceration, xi, 4, 77, 84, 93, 179; increased, in intermediate sanctions, 7, 8, 95, 103, 106; of intermediate sanctions, 8, 10, 12, 90–91, 93, 99–100, 106, 119–20, 126–28, 137, 146, 178–79; of probation, 93; of U.S. corrections system, 115

counseling: benefits of, 93, 94, 101, 154–55, 158–59; in boot camps, 145–47, 150, 154–55, 158–59; in day-reporting centers, 128–30, 132; in intensive supervision programs, 92–94, 100–101

crime: intermediate sanctions and rate of, 48–49; relation of

punishment to severity of, 3–4, 12–13, 95, 102–3, 170–72. *See also* deterrents; offenders; property crimes; punishment; violent crimes

Crime, Justice, and Protecting the Public (British white paper), 2

Crime and Justice Foundation, 128–29, 131

crime rates: in Germany, 48–49; in U.S.

Criminal Justice Act of 1991 (Great Britain), 18, 34, 36, 37, 116–17, 119, 120, 131, 135

criminal records, 50, 52, 55

CSOs. *See* community service orders

CSP. *See* client-specific planning

curfews, 89, 118–21, 128

day centres. *See* day-reporting centers

day fines, 16–17, 19–31; collection of, 17, 23–25, 27; community service as form of, 71; definition of, 5, 19; delinquent, 25–29; determination of, 16–17, 19, 20, 22–23, 27; target population for, 27–29; in U.S., 5, 17, 19–26; in western countries, xi–xii, 5–6, 16–17, 19–26. *See also* unit fines

day-reporting centers (DRCs), xii, 6, 103, 121, 124, 125–38; completion rates at, 127, 130–31; definition of, 128; in England, xii, 5, 124, 129, 131–38; goals of, 125, 126, 132, 134; privately operated, 126; and recidivism rates, 130–31, 136–37; target populations for, 126–28, 132, 134–35; in U.S., xii, 5, 121, 124, 125–30

Delaware, 175–77, 182

Denmark, 16

deterrents: community service orders as, 31; fines as, 19, 31–32; probation as, 31; short-term incarceration as, 144

Digital Products, 114

Index

Index

Index

National Institute of Justice, 26, 108, 126, 127, 140, 149

NCIA. *See* National Center on Institutions and Alternatives

Neilson, Judge Claud, 172, 174

"net-widening," 7–8, 70, 90, 114–15, 122, 179, 190

New Jersey, 5; intensive supervision programs in, 86–87, 89, 90

New Mexico, 59, 60, 186

New Mexico Center for Dispute Resolution, 60

New York: boot camps in, 122, 142–43, 145, 149, 154–59; community service programs in, 70, 74–77; day fines in, 5, 17, 20–26; probation caseloads in, 70–72

New Zealand, 73

nighttime confinement, 121

NIJ. *See* National Institute of Justice

North Carolina, 169, 172, 178

Northern Ireland, 116, 161–65

OCC. *See* Michigan Office of Community Corrections

offenders: female, 134–35; first-time, 123, 131, 144; group work with, 135; political, 161–65; reactions of, to boot camp, 123, 150–51, 555–56; reactions of, to community service orders, 81–84; sentencing of non-prison-bound, to intermediate sanctions, 7, 10, 86, 122, 144, 158, 200–201. *See also* employment; selection; target populations; traffic offenders

Office for Prisoner and Community Justice (Catholic Charities), 60

Ohio, 186

Oklahoma, 5, 149, 153

Oregon, 5; community corrections acts in, 185–88; day fines in, 21, 26, 29–30; intensive supervision programs in, 96–99

Overcrowded Times (journal), xi, xii, 36

overcrowding (of prisons), xi, 4, 94–95, 98–99, 106, 140–43, 147, 150, 184, 189; reduction in, 13, 113, 156–58

Panel on the Understanding and Control of Violent Behavior (National Academy of Sciences), 2

Parent, Dale, 8, 13, 122, 124

parole. *See* intensive supervision programs

Pennsylvania, 65–68, 182, 186

Petersilia, Joan, 13, 88, 91

placement. *See* sentencing

political prisoners, 161–65

political will, 13, 198–202

politicians: persuading, of soundness of day-reporting centers, 129; support for boot camps by, 122–23, 139, 145–46, 159; and support for community corrections, 198–202; support of, for incarceration, xi, 1–4, 11, 145–46. *See also* conservatives; liberals

presentence investigation reports (PSIs), 168–70

Pride, Inc., 114

prison. *See* incarceration

prisoners' rights movement, 184

private *vs.* public. *See* public *vs.* private

probation, 8, 138, 174; costs of, 31; in Germany, 44–45, 49; as intermediate sanction, 6, 92–94; origins of, 1; and recidivism rates, 69–70. *See also* intensive supervision programs; probation staff

probation centers. *See* day-reporting centers

probation staff: caseloads of, 70, 85, 89, 92, 126, 133–34, 167; at day-reporting centers, 133–34; funding of, 167, 169–70; intensive supervision contacts by, 85, 86,

Index